Peer Relationships in Early Childhood Education and Care

Peer Relationships in Early Childhood Education and Care brings together fresh perspectives and research about young children's relationships. It examines children's rights and well-being against a backdrop of increased social movement and migration, changing family structures and work practices, and the growing prevalence of education and care services for young children.

With contributors from diverse cultural, geographical and disciplinary backgrounds, this edited collection shows how educators support children's peer relationships and use these as a basis for enhancing social and cognitive development. Themes discussed include:

- conflicts and negotiations
- friendships and play
- group phenomena
- independence and interdependence
- identity and belonging
- peer relations and children with disabilities
- attuning adults to young children's relationships.

This book will be highly relevant for academics, researchers and students concerned with early childhood care and education, especially those interested in relating these issues on a global scale.

Margaret Kernan is Senior Programme Manager in International Child Development Initiatives (ICDI), the Netherlands.

Elly Singer is Associate Professor at the Department of Developmental Psychology, University of Utrecht and at the Faculty of Education of the University of Amsterdam, the Netherlands.

Peer Relationships in Early Childhood Education and Care

Edited by
Margaret Kernan and Elly Singer

LONDON AND NEW YORK

First edition published 2011
by Routledge
2 Park Square, Milton Park, Abingdon, Oxon OX14 4RN

Simultaneously published in the USA and Canada
by Routledge
270 Madison Avenue, New York, NY 10016

Routledge is an imprint of the Taylor & Francis Group, an informa business

Typeset in Perpetua by
Taylor & Francis Books
Printed and bound in Great Britain by
TJ International Ltd, Padstow

British Library Cataloguing in Publication Data
A catalogue record for this book is available from the British Library

Library of Congress Cataloging in Publication Data
Kernan, Margaret.
Peer relationships in early childhood education and care / Margaret Kernan and Elly Singer. – 1st ed.
p. cm.
Includes index.
1. Socialization. 2. Interpersonal relations in children – United States. 3. Early childhood education – United States. I. Singer, Elly, 1948–II. Title.
LC192.4.K44 2010
155.4'18 – dc22

2010004109

ISBN 978-0-415-57462-4 (hbk)
ISBN 978-0-415-57461-7 (pbk)
ISBN 978-0-203-84660-5 (ebk)

Acknowledgment is due to the Bernard van Leer Foundation for its financial support of the Community of Reflection and Practice on the Social Lives of Young Children, which led to this edited book.

Contents

Contributors

Nina von der Assen is Programme Manager at International Child Development Initiatives (ICDI), Leiden, The Netherlands. ICDI is an international non-governmental organisation, which works to promote the well-being of children growing up in difficult circumstances by assisting in the development of local capacity (of children, their communities, organizations, and authorities) to improve policies and practices. Nina's expertise includes children with disabilities and children's rights.

Carollee Howes' work and that of her colleagues at the University of California at Los Angeles (UCLA) has centred on children's development of social relationships within families and child care programmes. Los Angeles is the host location for the largest immigrant group in the United States, Mexican origin families, primarily from impoverished rural areas. It is also an international urban centre, which is diverse in social class, ethnicity, and home language.

Margaret Kernan has worked as a practitioner, trainer and researcher in early childhood education and care and primary education in Ireland, England and the Netherlands. A particular interest has been the role of play in children's lives at home, in care and educational settings and in the neighbourhood in urban settings. Margaret is a senior programme manager in International Child Development Initiatives (ICDI), Leiden, the Netherlands.

Anne Trine Kjørholt is Director of the Norwegian Centre for Child Research. She and her colleagues conduct research, which is theoretically and methodologically related to the paradigm of the interdisciplinary social studies of children and childhood. Among the recent larger research projects that Anne Trine is managing are: 1) The Modern Child and the Flexible Labour Market. Institutionalization and individualization of children's lives; 2) Children as Citizens and the Best Interest of the Child; 3) Children, Young People and Local Knowledge in Ethiopia and Zambia.

Bame Nsamenang's research interests are early childhood and youth development in context and Africa-sensitive teacher education textbook development. He is professor of psychology and learning science at the School of Education of the University of Yaoundé, Cameroon. He also directs the Human Development Resource Centre, a research and service facility.

Roxanna Pastor is Professor at the Mexican National Autonomous University (UNAM) Graduate School of Psychology, Mexico City, where she has been working with trainee psychologists who want to be early childhood specialists. Her work and those of her colleagues include assessment, evaluation and intervention from a developmental perspective with children, families, teachers and day care settings. Attention is paid to working directly with children, teachers, families and communities.

Sacha Powell, **Kathy Goouch** and **Tricia David** are members of the Early Childhood research community in the south east of England, based at Canterbury Christ Church University. Each team member has been involved in a wide range of research projects nationally and internationally. Individually they represent different specialisms and interests in the field of Early Childhood Education and Care, in particular: Sacha – children's rights; Kathy – literacy; Tricia – policy and practice. Collectively they seek to make research findings and responses to national policy accessible to a broad range of audiences and to demonstrate the importance of research in underpinning all our work with young children.

Miriam Rosenthal and **Lihi Gatt** are based in the Early Childhood Studies Department at the Hebrew University in Jerusalem. This university department has been highly involved for over 30 years in attempts to improve quality of care in Israeli day care through: research that documents different aspects of children's and staff experience in day care settings; the development of research-based training models and intervention programmes aiming at improving quality of care; and through attempts to change social policy related to child care.

Maria Clotilde Rossetti-Ferreira, **Zilma de Moraes Ramos de Oliveira**, **Mara Ignez Campos-de-Carvalho** and **Katia Souza Amorim** are researchers in the Brazilian Investigation Center on Human Development and Early Child Education (CINDEDI), which initiated its activities at the University of São Paulo in late seventies, became a formal institution in 1990s, and was recognized by UNESCO in 1996. The researchers in CINDEDI are involved in interrelated activities, such as research, training and education of human resources; consultation and guidance for day care centers and foster institutions; production of teaching materials and didactic-scientific videos, and lobby and advocacy on behalf of children and youth.

Elly Singer is Associate Professor at the University Utrecht and University of Amsterdam.

Dorian de Haan is Associate Professor at the University Utrecht and INHOLLAND University. They were involved in a wide range of studies of young children in group settings in the Netherlands focusing on gender and multicultural issues; joint play, humour and conflicts; (non)verbal communication and language development; teachers' roles and communication with the children. Elly is specialized in the history of early childhood education and care and in social emotional development.

Dorian is specialized in language development and language education. Both participate in projects to improve the pedagogical quality of Dutch child care centres.

Rita Swinnen joined the Dutch-based Bernard van Leer Foundation in 1985 as programme specialist responsible for programme development and project monitoring in a selected number of countries and regions. While functioning as programme officer in the issue area Social Inclusion & Respect for Diversity she took the initiative in 2007 to develop a community of reflection and practice on the social lives of young children. She left the Foundation in 2009 and is still active as an independent consultant in early childhood education.

Foreword

William A. Corsaro

When I began research on peer relations among pre-school children more than 35 years ago, I was much influenced by Piaget and Vygotsky and convinced that children *actively* contributed to their own social and emotional development. However, I also believed that these theorists (especially Piaget) underestimated the importance and abilities of pre-school children to collectively produce their own peer cultures. The best way to pursue this belief was to join a group of children and their teachers in a pre-school, to try to become one of the children as best I could, and observe and document what I found to be a vibrant and complex peer culture (Corsaro, 1985). I discovered many aspects of the children's peer culture, but two central themes stood out. The children made persistent attempts to *gain control* of their lives and always desired *to share* that control with each other.

The diverse and insightful chapters in *Peer Relationships in Early Childhood Education and Care* report research findings much in line with these themes of peer culture. They also contribute in important ways to the large and growing body of research on children's peer relations in early education settings. Firstly, the chapters tell us about *children's transition from the family* to the pre-school and children's adaptation to and participation in both a school and peer culture. Secondly, the chapters capture the importance of children's shared *collective agency* in these two cultures. Finally, the chapters draw our attention to the importance of the recognition and appreciation of *diversity* among the children, in the nature of childcare settings and institutions, and of the pedagogies and learning environments of pre-schools from a comparative perspective.

As more and more children enter childcare and early education (often even as infants and toddlers) the issue of transition has grown in importance. Young children seek, in adult caretakers and peers, the emotional bonds and feelings of security they first established in families. This striving to maintain a sense of security is most certainly a strong factor in children's valuing of participation, communal sharing and bonding in their peer cultures and friendship relations. Several of the chapters in this volume (Pastor Fasquelle; Howes; Kernan; Rosenthal and Gatt; and Singer and De Haan) impressively address important aspects of this transition process and how it can vary by age and cultural background of the children, the experience and training of teachers, and the pedagogy and organization of particular early education programmes.

A major theme in what has been termed the new paradigm of childhood studies is recognition of the importance of children's agency. This emphasis on children's agency can be seen in early childhood education programmes in Dahlberg's distinction between the *pre-primary tradition* and the *social pedagogic tradition*. The former stresses 'cognitive goals and readiness for formal school' while the latter stresses 'children's play and social development with an accent on children's agency' (Dahlberg, 2009: p. 229). Nearly all the chapters in this volume address children's agency to some degree, but it is most developed in chapters by David, Goouch and Powell; Kjørholt; and Nsamenang. Kjørholt in particular impressively discusses children's participatory rights and agency in line with the United Nations Convention on the Rights of the Child and how Norway has directly built these participatory rights into early education policy.

Finally, there is the importance of diversity, which is nicely captured in the diverse group of contributors to this volume and their views on peer relations in early education institutions and childcare settings. The range is extraordinary, from von der Assen and Kernan's incisive discussion of the rights of children with disabilities to develop and share close peer relations and friendships in inclusive pre-schools, to Rossetti-Ferreira, Ramos de Oliveira, Campos-de-Carvalho and Amorim's fine-grained analysis of the effects of spatial arrangements on the peer interactions of babies and toddlers in early childcare centres in Brazil, to Nsamenang's elegant narrative, which captures how 'African children are not only "certified" partners in caregiving and child protection but also significant contributors to family and community life.' Overall, the diversity and richness of this fine volume has much to offer to all of us who wish not just to educate children, but to enrich and appreciate their childhoods.

References

Corsaro, W.A. (1985) *Friendship and Peer Culture in the Early Years*. Norwood, N.J.: Ablex.

Dahlberg, G. (2009) 'Policies in early childhood education and care: potentialities for agency, play and learning'. In J. Qvortrup, W.A. Corsaro and M. Honig (eds) *The Palgrave Handbook of Childhood Studies*. Basingstoke, England: Palgrave.

Chapter 1

Introduction

Margaret Kernan, Elly Singer and Rita Swinnen

What this book is about

This book is about young children's relationships and children's active participation in their social world. An important premise is that the experience of positive social relations and the development of positive identities are core dimensions of children's well-being and sense of belonging (Brooker and Woodhead 2008; Bruner 2004; Dunn 2004). These are important concerns at a time when organized early childhood education and care settings have become significant sites of young children's daily lives in many contexts worldwide. Child rearing is increasingly acknowledged as a collaborative endeavour between families and early childhood education and care institutions (OECD 2006). Peer relationships are also a high priority for children because of the fun and pleasure they derive from being in the company of other children. This is often most evident in play.

Cross-cultural and historical studies show that non-parental care of young children was initially not designed to serve the needs of children (Lamb *et al.*1992). Non-parental early childhood arrangements have proliferated because parents need to be employed and cannot simultaneously care for their children. With economic need driving the demand, early childhood arrangements have been used in various countries to serve a variety of goals. These goals range from equal opportunities for males and females to acculturation of immigrants, rescuing young children 'at risk' from impoverished homes whose parents were considered incapable of effective socialization, and the provision of better educational opportunities for children from disadvantaged families (Lamb *et al.* 1992; Singer 1992). However, at the beginning of the 21st century, there is a growing trend to view early childhood education and care as a means to enrich the lives of all young children and their parents. Additionally, learning and thinking in the early years are increasingly being conceptualized as social activities. The growing influence of socio-cultural theories (Vygotsky 1978; Rogoff 2003) and relational pedagogy is reflected in the positioning of relationships and interactions at the heart of early childhood education and care curriculum frameworks in different regions throughout the world. For instance, in the national curriculum frameworks guiding practice in Ireland, the Netherlands, New Zealand and the countries of the UK, the role of exploration and play in young children's learning is stressed. Furthermore, young children's emotional security is seen as the result of the quality of the relationships between children, teachers and parents.

Phenomena such as urbanization, new patterns of migration and increased heterogeneity in societies, changing family structures and work practices are all impacting on children's everyday social experiences at home, and in early childhood education and care settings. These developments have created opportunities and challenges that require early years practitioners to think and act in new ways. This is reflected in the various chapters in this book. The bringing up of young children outside the family raises new questions about the educational values on which the pedagogy in early childhood settings should be based. In many countries early childhood education and care is beginning to be viewed within a children's rights framework due to the growing influence of the United Nations Convention on the Rights of the Child and the associated General Comment 7 on 'Implementing Child Rights in Early Childhood' (see for instance, Chapters 4 and 5). The pursuit of social justice, respect for diversity and ethical practices are emerging as core values in early childhood pedagogy (see Chapters 8 and 9). Increased attention is being paid to the development of respectful, partnership relations between early years practitioners and families and children; migrant parents' expectations and experiences of early childhood education and care settings (Adair and Tobin 2008; Prott and Hautumm 2005; Chapter 10); to identity and belonging (see Chapter 6); and to young children's active participation and the experience of citizenship (Kjørholt 2008). In these changing conditions, early childhood education and care assumes an important role in building and sustaining respectful communities.

Source: Copyright Project Singer 2007

The topic of 'young children's relationships' relates in this book to children's interpersonal relations with peers, younger and older children, and adults in their everyday lives, at home, and in the whole host of early childhood care and education settings, 'organized' or less 'organized', where young children from birth to 8 years spend their time. It encompasses understandings and experiences of nurturance, care and learning in interactions and interpersonal relations; conflicts and negotiation; pleasure and rejection; friendships and play; group phenomena; independence and interdependence; and identity and belonging. Our particular interest in this book is in children's 'lived through experience' (Valsiner 2007) of social relations in the niche of their everyday lives, acknowledging the cultural and contextual diversity of childhood and children's lives globally – and therefore the many forms that social relationships may take, and the meanings that may be attributed to them (see Chapters 3 and 7). Our aim in this book is also to explore questions relating to social justice and community building through the lens of young children's relationships in early childhood education and settings.

Children's perspectives on their social relationships

Relationships and interactions, particularly interactions between early childhood practitioners and children, have been identified as a key element of process quality in early childhood education and care (Howes and James 2002) and significant for positive outcomes for children (OECD 2001; Shonkoff and Phillips 2000). Consequently, in recent decades considerable attention has been paid to researching and describing optimal adult–child relationships in early childhood pedagogy (Ebbeck and Yim 2008; Papatheodorou and Moyles 2009). Somewhat less attention is being paid to understanding young children's relationships and interactions with other children in terms of what children 'get' from relationships (Rubin, Bukowski and Parker 2006). Relationships and friendships matter to children. As noted by Dunn (2004: 3) 'We are missing a major piece of what excites, pleases, and upsets children, what is central to their lives even in the years before school, if we don't attend to what happens between children and their friends'. The priority children give to their peer relationships, often encapsulated in 'playing together', is evident when young children are consulted about what is important in their everyday lives in early childhood education and care settings (Clark and Moss 2001; Corsaro 2004; Moromizato 2008). It is also apparent in the narratives of older children when they recall their early childhood (Torstenson-Ed 2007).

Distinguishing different types of social relationships

In early childhood education and care settings young children enter into two different types of relationships: those formed with adults and those formed with peers (Singer and de Haan 2007). From a very young age children differentiate between these two types. They rely on adults for emotional support, security, practical help, cognitive challenges, moral rules and guidance. Parents and teachers structure young children's

Source: Copyright Project Singer 2007

lives in many ways. They let them participate in routines and rituals; they organize the material environment and time; they teach 'dos' and 'don'ts'. Parents and teachers guide young children often with an 'invisible' hand with help of structured patterns of behaviour, time structures and an organized physical environment. With peers, young children enter into more equal relationships. Young children are attractive social partners for each other because of shared interests, excitement and joy in play activities. When young children meet each other on a regular basis they co-construct shared meanings, expectations and rituals. They develop friendships and a peer culture. According to Corsaro (2004) young children co-construct in recurrent interactions shared meanings, humour, conflict strategies and games in which they incorporate elements of the adults' culture. In the peer group they appropriate, in their own way, what they understand and learn from their teachers and parents. For teachers it is important to understand both types of relationships. They should make room for the rituals and expectations peers co-construct among themselves alongside the rituals, routines and rules of the adults in the home and the centre. See Figure 1.1.

To support children in adapting to the social life in the childcare group, teachers need to be aware of different levels of social dynamics. Firstly, there is the level of the dyadic relationship of the teacher and the individual child: that is, the interaction of the teacher with an individual child (Chapter 2). Research based on the attachment

Source: Copyright Project Singer 2007

theory shows that availability and sensitive responses of the teacher to the child's signals fosters the emotional security of the child. Especially for new children in the group, physical proximity to the teacher is often very important. Later on they rely more on social referencing while they are playing alone or with peers at some distance from the teacher (Hoogdalem *et al.* 2008). They are regularly looking at the teacher – 'is she still taking care of me?' Young children read the emotional expressions on the teacher's face – 'is what I do okay?' Teachers often react to the child's social referencing by giving short verbal and non-verbal signs. So they monitor the child's behaviour from a distance and create psychological closeness without being physically nearby.

Secondly, teachers help children to adapt to the social life in the group at the level of dyadic peer relationships and subgroups. From the moment children develop the motor skills to move around freely, they show interest in other children. During free play they spend much more time with peers than with a teacher (Singer and de Haan 2007). With peers, young children quickly learn that they are challenged to improvise and to cope with misunderstandings and disagreements. Most children like to play with peers. But in every group there are children who have problems adapting themselves to group life. Without the support of the teacher these children become the isolated and neglected children of the group. Sometimes the impulsive children with many conflicts become the scapegoats of the group and are blamed for all the

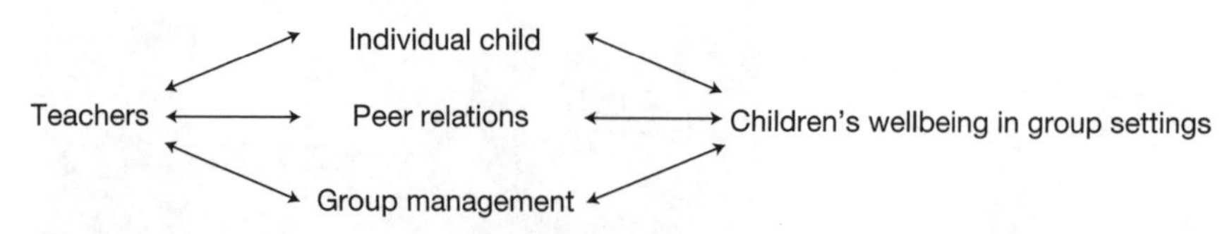

Figure 1.1 Three levels of teacher's support.

aggressive actions and crying that may occur during peer conflicts (Singer and de Haan 2007). In peer relations children discover that they have influence and that they can play and experiment with power – in a positive way by helping other children and showing leadership behaviour, and in a negative way by bullying peers. For instance a girl, almost four years old, the oldest of the group and well liked by the teachers in a Dutch early childhood education and care setting, had discovered that she could kick a younger boy without being observed by the teacher; when the boy reacted by hitting her, he was blamed and not she. It took some time before the teachers discovered the real 'perpetrator' and could regulate and discuss this behaviour with the children.

Thirdly, there is the level of dynamics in the whole group and between subgroups (Vaughn and Santos 2008). At this level teachers manage the children in order to foster positive relationships between all the children (Ahnert *et al.* 2006). They organize the rooms inside and outside so the children can play without disturbing each other. They have a balanced play activity plan and time schedule that matches the needs of the children. Besides that, they organize at various points during the day group activities in which all children are invited to participate. For instance: circle time; singing songs during tidying up or before lunch; dancing together; rituals related to birthdays or to welcome new children. When children are new in the group, the teachers scaffold them in the routines, rituals and rules of the group. They foster 'we-feelings' and a sense of belonging in the group.

Developing a new field of research

For a long time research neglected the complexity of children's social relations in groups. Until recently, most knowledge of young children was based on theories that were implicitly rooted in a pedagogical concept of family upbringing (Singer 1992). Mother–child interactions have been one of the most studied issues in developmental psychology, particularly within the framework of attachment theory (NICHD 1997). According to attachment theory the child needs a sensitive and responsive mother for the development of a healthy bond and emotional security. Attachment theory was also influential in the context of early childhood education and care centres and led to an exclusive focus on teacher–child interactions. Subsequently, researchers and practitioners acknowledged that attachment theory was too narrow to capture the relational complexities in early childhood education and care settings. In these settings children relate to two or more teachers, instead of to one mother at home; the parents and the teachers have to cooperate, and the children meet peers. The authors of this book all agree that the attachment theory, with an exclusive focus on the dyadic mother–child relationship, is not enough. They have broadened attachment theory (Chapter 2) or looked for alternative theoretical approaches (Chapters 7, 8 and 10).

In contrast to the focus on the mother–child relationship, mainstream developmental psychology hardly paid any attention to the peer relations of young children. Until the 1990s, the peer relations of young children were considered to be rare, short-lived and often aggressive (Schaffer 1984). That opinion was based on hardly any research. However, group care of young children in organized childhood education services opened up new opportunities for studying peer relations in natural settings. At the same time, early years practitioners were developing skills and knowledge relating to peer interactions and relationships through their everyday work with young children in group settings. Significantly, a small but distinct body of knowledge relating to social relations in group settings, which was located primarily within the fields of developmental psychology and child development, soon followed in many different locations in Europe and the United States. For instance, in the United States, Howes (1988) was one of the first researchers to study factors that influence peer relations and friendships of young children. In Europe, innovative research on this topic was being conducted by the CRESAS in Paris (Centre de Recherches de Éducation et de l'Adaption Scolaire), often in cooperation with Italian researchers such as Bonica and Mussatti (Stambak and Sinclair 1993). In the former East Germany, the Nordic countries and the Netherlands, (small) groups of researchers were also doing innovative work in this field (Ahnert *et al.* 2000; Hännikäinen 1999; Løkken 2000; Singer and de Haan 2007). Because of language barriers, these studies have only recently become available to an international audience (Lamb *et al.* 1992). While the vast majority of published research literature on children's social relationships related to studies in N. America and Europe, it is also noteworthy that similar research was being conducted in a range of out-of-home settings in Brazil (Ramos de Oliveira and Rossetti-Ferreira 1996) and Israel (Rosenthal 1999).

Research topics have included: peer interaction of young children in naturalistic settings (Howes 1988); children's friendships (Dunn 2004); play, peer relationships and social development (Rubin, Bukowski and Parker 2006); sibling relationships (Dunn 1993); humour (Loizou 2005); peer imitation and cognitive development (Hanna and Meltzoff 1993); and ethology and the study of group dynamics (Vaughn and Santos 2008).

By the 1990s, sociological studies of children's peer cultures also began to be published (Deegan 1996; Corsaro 2004; Mayall 2002). By utilising a range of qualitative and ethnographic methodologies, including participant observation and interviewing, these researchers studied how children's relationships were experienced and understood by children. They also sought to capture the 'real world' experiences of children, including the flow and the complexities of peer relationships in group settings such as early childhood education and care and primary schools.

The emergence of the broader field of social studies of childhood brought with it an increased awareness of diverse cultural and cross-cultural meanings relating to social relationships as well as the recognition that children are a primary source of knowledge about their experiences. Early childhood education and care practice began to be informed by a more multidisciplinary research base and greater attention began to be paid to the plurality of childhoods, evidenced cross-culturally (Lamb *et al.* 1992; Rogoff 2003; Woodhead *et al.* 1998), but also within cultures and societies (Genishi and Goodwin 2008; Tudge 2008) as well as to children's perspectives regarding what is important to them in their daily lives in early childhood education and care.

All these developments necessitate further reflection and debate regarding the changing characteristics and contexts of young children's social relationships in different societies and cultures around the globe and how they impact on everyday practice in early childhood education and care.

A community of reflection and practice on the social lives of young children

In October 2008, a group of 12 researchers from Africa, Asia, Europe, North, South and Meso America came together to share their expertise on the topic of the social lives of young children and to learn from each other's experiences. The themes and guiding questions for the meeting were derived both from research conducted by the participants as well as work of key researchers from diverse countries.

A number of core premises set the context for the deliberations. These included: (1) peer relationships and friendships matter to children; (2) the need to belong and to experience reciprocated friendships is universal – although there may be a diversity in how togetherness and belonging are expressed; (3) peer relationships are central to all children's well-being and positive identity; (4) there are different ways of knowing and in thinking about children's peer relationships – there is a need to create space for social and cultural context-bound insights.

The wide range of contributions at the meeting encompassed diverse methodologies, paradigms, discourses, languages, ways of viewing from sociological, anthropological, cultural psychological perspectives as well as from developmental psychological, ethological, child development and early childhood educational perspectives. Participants grappled with issues such as how participation, autonomy and interdependence could best be understood in the context of peer relations in group settings; accessing children's perspectives of peer relations in daily practice; who decides how long, with whom, what or where to play and the kinds of approaches and interventions that are most effective in instigating positive change in practitioners' responsivity and sensitivity to the social lives of the children they work with.

Evidence presented was rigorous, authentic (within its own context) and empirically based, and gave voice to many perspectives and from multiple cultural contexts. In the ensuing lively discussions, beliefs, values and meanings were elaborated, and dilemmas and solutions to common problems were shared and debated. This book is the outcome of the Community of Reflection and Practice process.

Organisation of the book

We begin with a chapter by Carollee Howes, in which she describes a theoretical framework she developed to understand peer relationships among young children in

North American multicultural contexts. This framework takes into account children's home cultural community, their relationship history and peer group history, as well as their dispositions and communicative ability. A central part of the framework is the social and emotional climate of the early childhood programme where young children spend their time. Howes (Chapter 2) expresses concern that young children have fewer opportunities to play freely together in early years services, due to the downward pressure of teacher-directed academic learning. This concern about young children's opportunities to play with peers is shared by the authors of the following three chapters.

The chapter by Kernan (Chapter 3), which draws on a number of studies conducted in Ireland, illustrates that space and time to play with peers provide rich learning opportunities for children about themselves and their relations with others. This may not always be a pleasurable experience. Many children have to learn how to deal with being excluded or bullied, and struggle in their attempts to form friendships and feel a sense of belonging to the peer group. Such negative experiences underscore the importance to take into account young children's concerns. Children's perspectives are also prioritized by Anne Trine Kjørholt in Chapter 4. The background of her chapter is the United Nations Convention on the Rights of the Child and the notion of child participation. She critiques the implicit emphasis in the educational policy and practice in the Nordic countries on individual autonomy, self-determination and verbal expression when considering children's participation rights. Kjørholt offers an alternative perspective, which prioritizes relational aspects to children's participation including their playfulness with each other, joint bodily movements and emotional meaning-making processes. The authors of Chapter 5, Tricia David, Kathy Goouch and Sacha Powell, examine the position of play in early childhood in the policy context in England. They point at the dual role of teachers. On the one hand teachers have to work with performance indicators, learning goals and records of achievement; on the other hand they have to work within a policy framework for the early years, which purports to emphasize the importance of free play. In this chapter, David *et al.* discuss how practitioners deal with apparently conflicting demands and argue that it is possible to address educational aims 'through enabling young children to play, to express themselves, to make choices, develop agency and autonomy and by helping them to make and sustain friendships'.

In Chapters 6 to 9 the reader is introduced to more in-depth studies of peer relationships in contrasting contexts in different parts of the world. Bame Nsamenang, in Chapter 6, focuses on rural areas in Cameroon in West Africa where young children spend time with older children in mixed aged groups outside institutional settings, and where older children have delegated responsibility to care for and supervise younger children. Here, as the photographs included in this chapter illustrate, all children participate in adult work at their own level. However, Nsamenang notes that as more children in Cameroon spend more time in institutionalized settings, this form of peer culture is changing. He concludes by pleading for the incorporation of a 'participative spirit, child-to-child sociability and self-generation of peer cultures' in institutionalized early years settings. Chapter 7 brings the reader to Brazil, a country where institutionalized group care is also a relatively new phenomenon. In the aftermath of the military dictatorship between the 1960s and 1980s, during which an authoritarian culture dominated, services struggled to provide quality care and education experiences to all young children in settings that were organized in same-age groups. In response, Rossetti-Ferreira and her colleagues at the Brazilian Investigation Center on Human Development and Early Childhood Education (CINDEDI) developed a new way of looking at and understanding peer relationships between babies, toddlers and pre-school aged children. One of the prime methodologies used by Rossetti-Ferreira and her colleagues was video analysis.

In Chapters 8 and 9, peer relations are discussed with respect to diversity among young children. Elly Singer and Dorian de Haan studied peer relations among two- and three-year-olds in multicultural daycare centres in the Netherlands. They describe how conflicts and disagreements were used as a lens to achieve better understanding of processes in children's peer relations. One of the issues raised in their chapter is that while toddlers are very dependent on adult support as they learn to co-construct shared meanings, inappropriate adult interventions can also endanger peer relations. While Singer and de Haan did not find differences between different cultural groups in terms of social skills in peer relations, interviews with parents indicated that there was mutual misunderstanding between groups regarding beliefs and child-rearing behaviours. They recommend focusing on similarities and shared challenges in multicultural settings and conclude that childcare centres can play an important role in community building in multicultural societies. In Chapter 9, the focus is on the rights of children with disabilities to have satisfying play and peer relationships, just as their non-disabled peers. In this chapter Nina von der Assen and Margaret Kernan focus particularly on research that has examined children's experiences of peer relations in inclusive settings, that is settings in which children with and without disabilities participate in the same group. As noted by the authors, this is both an ethical and pedagogical issue. For inclusion to be successful, attention needs to be paid to the particular strategies and supports adults can employ to support the development of social skills of all children in inclusive settings.

In the final two chapters, accounts are provided of two training programmes that have been developed to enhance practitioners' skills in supporting children's socio-emotional development. The context of Chapter 10 is Israel. Here Miriam Rosenthal and Lihi Gatt have been responsible for the development of the 'Learning to Live Together' programme. The caregivers participating in the programme learn how to transform the childcare setting into an environment in which children acquire patterns of considerate, respectful and empathetic interpersonal relations. According to Rosenthal and Gatt, it is not sufficient to instruct caregivers to 'respond sensitively'. Rather, this programme trains practitioners in a variety of specific interventions that can be used during the various naturally occurring emotional and social events in a group of young children. In common with a number of other authors in this book, Rosenthal and Gatt also point to the importance of practitioners being aware of, and critically reflecting on, their personal and culturally based attitudes and beliefs concerning social behaviours and development (see also Howes, Chapter 2; Kjørholt, Chapter 4; Singer and de Haan, Chapter 8). Learning to critically reflect on your own preconceived notions is also a key component of the practice-based training programme that has been developed by Roxanna Pastor Fasquelle in collaboration with postgraduate students in the Mexican National Autonomous University (UNAM), Mexico City. This programme brings together trainee mentors and advisers (educational psychology students) with very basically trained childcare providers in joint learning and professional development. In Chapter 11, Pastor Fasquelle draws attention to the importance of respect, listening, humility and a non-judgemental approach in learning. This applies whether we are talking about adults or children learning. The slogan of the last two chapters in the context of this book could be: practise what you preach. In other words, as trainers and mentors we need to show respect for the teachers' perspectives, their concerns and cultural backgrounds, just as we wish them to show respect for children's concerns, including their interest in playing with peers and their need for trustworthy teachers.

In conclusion

One of the strengths of the book and its collection of contributing authors is the diverse disciplinary and cultural contexts represented. In this regard a note on terminology is necessary. Throughout this introductory chapter we have used the term 'early childhood education and care' to describe the range of settings outside the family home where young children spend their time. But in different disciplinary and cultural contexts different terminology is used. As editors, we have strived to achieve balance between consistency within and across chapters on the one hand, and maintaining diversity and context-sensitive terminology on the other hand. The common

Source: Copyright Jon Spaull/Bernard van Leer Foundation

thread running through these diverse contributions is that group settings for young children can have an important educational value and that children value highly contacts with peers and friendship. We hope the readers will be inspired and encouraged to engage in critical reflection to build up creative communities of playing and learning children and adults.

Bibliography

Adair, J. and Tobin, J. (2008) 'Listening to the voice of immigrant parents'. In C. Genishi and L. Goodwin (eds) *Diversities in Early Childhood Education: Rethinking and Doing*. New York: Routledge.

Ahnert, L., Lamb, M.E. and Seltenheim, K. (2000) 'Infant–care provider attachments in contrasting child care settings I: Group-oriented care before German reunification'. *Infant Behavior and Development,* 23: 197–209.

Ahnert, L., Pinquart, M. and Lamb, M.E. (2006) 'Security of children's relationships with non-parental care providers: a meta-analysis'. *Child Development*, 74: 664–79.

Brooker, L. and Woodhead, M. (eds) (2008) *Developing Positive Identities: Diversity and Young Children.* Milton Keynes: The Open University with support from the Bernard van Leer Foundation.

Bruner, J. (2004) 'Foreword'. In J. Dunn, *Children's Friendships: the Beginnings of Intimacy.* Oxford: Blackwell, pp. vi-vii.

Clark, A. and Moss, P. (2001) *Listening to Young Children: the Mosaic Approach.* London: National Children's Bureau.

Corsaro, W. (2004) *The Sociology of Childhood*, second edition. Thousand Oaks, C.A.: Pine Forge Press.

Deegan, J.G. (1996) *Children's Friendships in Culturally Diverse Classrooms.* London: Falmer Press.

Dunn, J. (1993) *Young Children's Close Relationships: Beyond Attachment.* London: Sage.

——(2004) *Children's Friendships: the Beginnings of Intimacy.* Oxford: Blackwell.

Ebbeck, M. and Yim, H.Y.B. (2008) 'Fostering relationships between infants, toddlers and their primary caregivers in childcare centres in Australia'. In M.R. Jalongo (ed) *Enduring Bonds: The Significance of Interpersonal Relations in Young Children's Lives.* New York: Springer.

Genishi, C. and Goodwin, A.L. (eds) (2008) *Diversities in Early Childhood Education: Rethinking and Doing.* New York: Routledge.

Hanna, E. and Meltzoff, A.N. (1993) 'Peer imitation by toddlers in laboratory, home, and day-care contexts: implication for social learning and memory'. *Developmental Psychology,* 29: 701–10.

Hännikäinen, M. (1999) 'Togetherness. A manifestation of early day care life'. *Early Child Development and Care,* 151: 19–28.

Hoogdalem, A., Singer, E., Streck, L. and Bekkema, N. (2008) 'Young children who intervene in peer conflicts in multicultural child care centers'. *Behaviour,* 145: 1653–70.

Howes, C. (1988) 'Peer Interaction in Young Children'. *Monograph of the Society for Research in Child Development*, 217(53): 1.

Howes, C. and James, J. (2002) 'Children's social development within the socialization context of childcare and early childhood education'. In P.K. Smith and C.H. Hart (eds) *Blackwell Handbook of Childhood Social Development.* Oxford: Blackwell.

Kjørholt, A.-T. (2008) 'Children as new citizens: in the best interests of the child?'. In A. James and A.L. James (eds) *European Childhoods: Cultures, Politics and Childhoods in Europe.* New York: Palgrave Macmillan.

Lamb, M.E. Sternberg, K.J. Hwang, C.-P. and Broberg, A.G. (eds) (1992) *Child Care in Context: Cross-Cultural Perspectives.* Hillsdale, New Jersey: Lawrence Erlbaum.

Loizou, E. (2005) 'Infant humor: the theory of the absurd and the empowerment theory'. *International Journal of Early Years Education,* 13: 43–53.

Løkken, G. (2000) 'Tracing the social style of toddler peers'. *Scandinavian Journal of Educational Research,* 46: 163–77.

Mayall, B. (2002) *Towards a Sociology for Childhood: Thinking From Children's Lives.* Buckingham: Open University Press.

Moromizato, R. (2008) 'Building bridges: quality in successful transition between families and schools in the central rainforest of Peru'. *Early Childhood Matters,* 110: 35–8

National Institute for Child Health and Development (NICHD), Early Child Care Research Network (1997) 'The effects of infant care on infant–mother attachment security: results of the NICHD-Study of Early Child Care'. *Child Development,* 68: 860–79.

OECD (2001) *Starting Strong: Early Childhood Education and Care.* Paris: Organisation for Economic Co-operation and Development.

——(2006) *Starting Strong II.* Paris: Organisation for Economic Co-operation and Development.

Oliveira, Z.M.R. and Rossetti-Ferreira, M.C. (1996) 'Understanding the co-constructive nature of human development: role co-ordination in early peer interaction'. In J. Valsiner and H-G. Voss (eds) *The Structure of Learning Processes.* Norwood, N.J.: Ablex.

Papatheodorou, T. and Moyles, J. (eds) (2009) *Learning Together in the Early Years: Exploring Relational Pedagogy.* Abingdon: Routledge.

Prott, R. and Hautumm, A. (2005) *12 Principles for Successful Cooperation between Childcare Workers and Parents.* Amsterdam: SWP Publishers.

Rogoff, B. (2003) *The Cultural Nature of Human Development.* Oxford: Oxford University Press.

Rosenthal, M. (1999) 'Out-of-home child care research: a cultural perspective'. *International Journal of Behavioural Development,* 23: 477–518.

Rubin, K.H., Bukowski, W.M. and Parker, J.G. (2006) 'Peer interactions, relationships and groups'. In W. Damon and N. Eisenberg (eds) *Social, Emotional and Personality Development, Handbook of Child Psychology.* New York: Wiley.

Schaffer, H.R. (1984) *The Child's Entry into a Social World.* London: Academic Press.

Shonkoff, J.P. and Phillips, D.A. (2000) *From Neurons to Neighbourhoods: the Science of Early Childhood Development.* Washington, D.C.: National Academy Press.

Singer, E. (1992) *Child Care and the Psychology of Development.* London/New York: Routledge.

Singer, E. and de Haan, D. (2007) 'Social life of young children. Co-construction of shared meanings and togetherness, humour, and conflicts in child care centers'. In B. Spodek and O.N. Saracho (eds), *Contemporary Perspectives on Research in Early Childhood Social Learning.* Charlotte, N.C.: Information Age Publishers.

Stambak, M., and Sinclair, H. (1993) *Pretend Play Among 3 Year Olds.* Hillsdale, N.J.: Erlbaum.

Torstenson-Ed, T. (2007) 'Children's life paths through preschool and school: letting youths talk about their own childhood – theoretical and methodological conclusions'. *Childhood,* 14: 47–66.

Tudge, J. (2008) *The Everyday Lives of Young Children: Culture, Class, and Child Rearing in Diverse Societies.* Cambridge: Cambridge University Press.

Valsiner, J. (2007) *Culture in Minds and Societies: Foundations of Cultural Psychology.* New Delhi: Sage.

Vaughn, B.E. and Santos, A.J. (2008) 'Structural descriptions of social transactions among young children: affiliation and dominance in preschool groups'. In K.H. Rubin, W. Bukowski and B. Laursen (eds), *Handbook of Peer Interactions, Relationships, and Groups.* New York: Guilford Press.

Vygotsky, L.S. (1978) *Mind in Society. The Development of Higher Psychological Processes.* Cambridge, M.A.: Harvard University Press.

Woodhead, M., Faulker, D. and Littleton, K. (1998) *Cultural Worlds of Early Childhood.* London: Routledge.

Chapter 2

A model for studying socialization in early childhood education and care settings

Carollee Howes[1]

Introducing the theoretical framework

In order to understand and interpret the importance of peer relations of young children I use a theoretical framework that integrates theories of children's development of social relationships with theories of development within context, most particularly within cultural communities. Understanding peer relations and their significance requires attention to individuals, dyads (pairs), peer and classroom groupings, and to cultural communities, including beliefs, values and norms. My theory of culture developmental interface is depicted in Figure 2.1

This graphic representation of culture developmental interface guides my understandings of the children's development of relations with peers. In order to explain children's development of social skills and relationships we must first account for dispositions and histories that the child brings to peer interaction. Children differ in temperament, some are shy and others exuberant in their peer encounters. Children also differ in their communicative abilities, verbal, non-verbal and emotional decoding. These individual differences in temperament and in communication skills influence their peer encounters (Dunn 2004; Justice *et al.* 2008; Spinrad *et al.* 2004). Children bring to their current encounters with peers varying experiences with interactions and relationships with parents and other significant adults (Howes and Spieker 2008) as well as their previous experiences with peers. The meanings and understandings that children derive from these experiences are brought to their peer encounters. Additionally, the interactions and relationships with peers are formed against the background of the children's home cultural community, depicted in the left-hand column of Figure 2.1.

Growing up in cultural communities

A cultural community is defined as a grouping of people who share goals, beliefs and everyday practices, and often a racial or ethnic identity (Rogoff 2003). Children and adults who participate in the same cultural community develop, through common activities and practices, social interaction forms and styles. For example in some cultural communities, but not all, dinner table conversations or bedtime stories are times

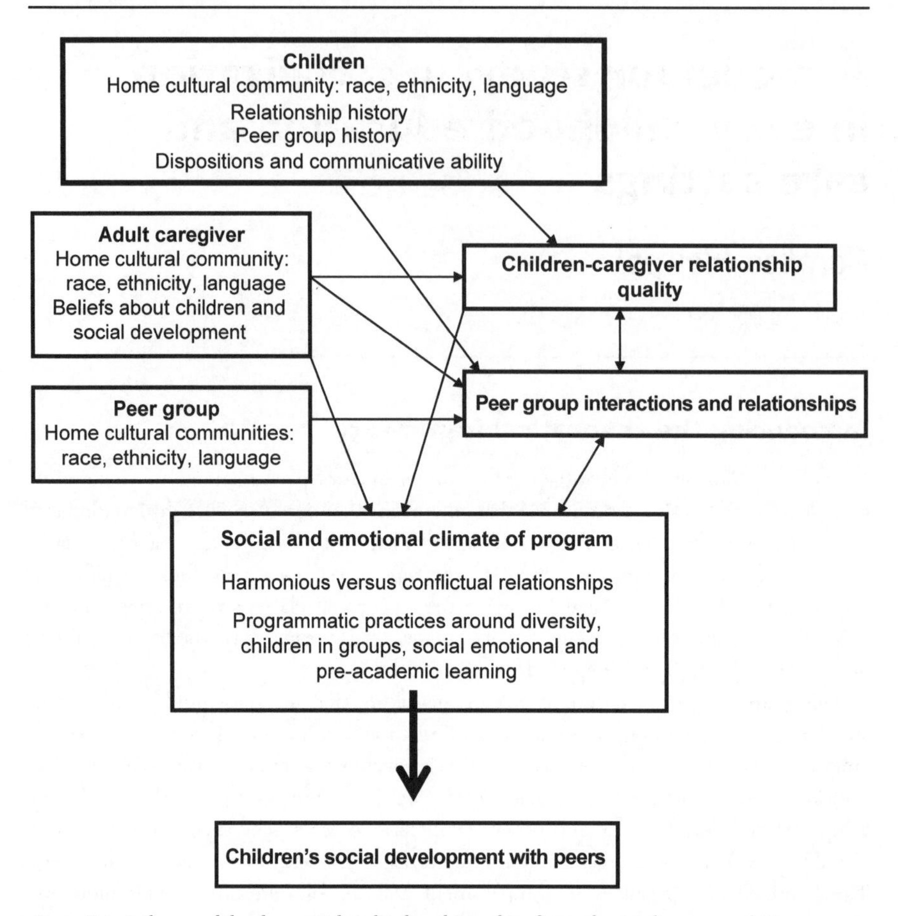

Figure 2.1 A theory of developmental and cultural interface for understanding peer relations.

that children and their parent co-create narratives of the day's experiences. By participation in everyday activities, such as these dinner table conversations, children develop styles of social interaction that are particular to their cultural community. In one cultural community the 'way things are done' is to interrupt the speaker to elaborate a fantasy story, 'And then the little girl found a really big elephant just sitting in the back yard … ' and in another it would be rude to interrupt and even worse to make up an untruth. Children and adults may find it relatively easy to identify practices and interactive styles that are different, and almost impossible to identify their way of doing as particular to themselves. Differences in practices and interactive styles may be in even sharper contrast when the home language of the cultural communities is different, i.e. Spanish at home and English with peers.

It is important to understand that cultural communities are dynamic, the experiences of each of the members of the cultural community influences their participation with other members of the cultural community and as a result activities and practices, and ways of thinking about activities and practices change. Therefore, as a result of parents and children participating in social interaction and relationship construction with adults and children outside of the home, home cultural community activities, practices and beliefs may change. For example, children in Spanish monolingual households often bring pretend play themes and English home from peer play, and share them with their younger siblings.

The adult caregivers who supervise children's play with peers also participate in cultural communities. Their home cultural communities function much as the children's home cultural communities, providing the adults with understandings, ways of doing things, and an interactive style and home language to use when engaging with others. This home cultural community may be the same or different from the home cultural communities of the children in the peer group. These similarities and differences may influence the relationships and interactions co-constructed by children and adults in the programme (Howes and Shivers 2006). Adult caregivers in peer settings also participate in a cultural community of the programme, carrying out activities and practices that are consistent with their beliefs around caring for children and helping them develop (Huijbregts *et al.* 2008; Wishard *et al.* 2003). These practices, for example what teachers do and say when children are excluded from play, as well as their interactions and relationships with children, shape the social development of children with their peers.

Considering the race, ethnicity and class of caregivers

Adult caregivers in childcare settings participate in cultural communities with various class and/or race and ethnicity identities. While childcare caregivers are generally better educated than other women workers, they are paid far less than similarly educated workers, which makes childcare workers' class position ambiguous. One line of research suggests that to the extent that adult caregivers in childcare settings are exposed to formal education and training in early childhood education, they may adopt values and/or social interactive styles that are associated with White middle class interactive styles (Lubeck 1996). If so, discontinuities between home and school social interactive styles may make it difficult for children (and their parents) (Baker, Terry, Bridger and Winsor 1997). Instead of feeling safe, children may feel out of place, unwanted or not sure about how to behave and whom to trust.

As part of a larger project that explores race, ethnicity and childcare quality we have conducted case studies on 12 centre-based childcare programmes that are respected in their communities for providing services to families and children who are low income and predominantly children of colour (Howes 2009). We were interested in examining the very specific ways that children spend their time during the day, and the interactions they had with adults and peers. We wanted to know who the staff were that were working with the children, specifically what motivated them to become caregivers, and what their attitudes were towards working with families. We wanted to look at the mission and focus of each centre. In line with the need to capture content inside of context, we incorporated a mixed method approach by interviewing staff and observing and participating in the classrooms of these centres.

Seventy staff members (66 women; 59 teaching staff) participated in this study. Forty per cent of the programme directors were African-American, 30 per cent Latino, and 30 per cent White. Fifty-five per cent of the teaching staff were Latino, 26 per cent African-American. The others were White, Asian or bi-racial. All of the teaching staff was highly educated in child development: 83 per cent of the directors had MA or Ph.D. degrees; 55 per cent of the head caregivers had BA degrees; and 79 per cent of the assistants had AA (Associate) degrees. From our ethnographic work, seven different categories of programme philosophy emerged, ranging from providing a safe environment and positive trusting social relationships, through helping young children understand and appreciate differences based in race, gender or disability, to providing academic preparation for school. We created, based on staff interviews, categories of caregivers' motivation to teach. Caregivers who report being motivated for the community see themselves as self-consciously involving themselves in their work in order to transform their own community into a community of which they wish to be a part. In contrast, caregivers that are motivated for the children gain little for themselves because their efforts are always for the children, children not necessarily from the caregiver's 'heritage' community, but children from all communities. Caregivers of every ethnic, racial and educational background ascribed to each of the programme philosophies and motivations to teach.

Using our observational data, we examined differences in caregivers' behaviours with the children based on caregiver ethnicity, educational background, motivation to teach and programme mission. We found that while an association between ethnicity and educational background existed, teaching motivation and programme missions better explained the differences in behaviours.

These findings suggest that while socialization for social development within childcare is embedded within race and ethnicity, individual variations in motivation to teach and to provide services for children are equally important to consider. Having said this, there were again subtle stylistic differences particular to race and ethnicity. For example, African-American caregivers invoked the construct of other-mothers, the notion that women who are not children's biological parents are responsible for the well-being of children who are not otherwise receiving adequate care and attention. While Latino caregivers talked about creating an extended family that took care of women and the children associated with them.

Adult caregivers' expectations of gendered behaviour also vary by their home and childcare centre cultural community. Childcare settings of course include both girls and boys at a period in development important for the acquisition of gendered behaviour styles. Adult caregivers in childcare settings vary in their use of gender as an organizing category within the programme. In two of our case study programmes children as young as two years old must form lines based on gender, and be careful not to use the bathroom of the opposite sex. In one of these programmes, girls and boys wear different uniforms, and the girls are in skirts or jumpers. And in another the roles in a pre-literacy activity involving acting out fairy tales are carefully assigned to the appropriate gender children. This is in dramatic contrast to another programme that has fully implemented the National Association for the Education of Young Children's Anti-Bias

Curriculum (Derman-Sparks 1989) and actively corrects children and adults who consciously or inadvertently attempt to impose traditional sex role behaviours on children as well as highlights when children or adults behave outside of predetermined roles. Yet another programme delights in its well equipped dramatic play area and energetically encourages girls to pretend to be plumbers and boys to take care of the babies.

Finally, rarely are all the children in the peer group the same or even similar in home cultural communities. Children in the programme may not all speak the same home language and may come from homes with different ideas and expectations about how to engage with others, for example to share materials or not to share. Constructing interactions and relationships among children from different home cultural communities may require different skills or different adult support than when all children are similar (Howes and Lee 2007).

Variations in children's relationships with adults and peers

The right-hand column of Figure 2.1 probably looks quite familiar to developmental psychologists. Children bring dispositions and skills: sociability and wariness, emotional regulation and communicative skills, that influence their construction of an attachment relationship with the adult caregiver (Howes and Spieker 2008) and their interactions and friendships with peers (Howes 2008). Positive attachment relationships with caregivers influences children's formation of positive relationships with peers (Howes 2008) and children who are in less conflict with peers are more likely to form positive relationships with caregivers (Howes and Shivers 2006).

Interactions with peers and relationships with peers (whether friendships or playmate relationships) develop through multiple and recursive interactive experiences. Recursive interactions are well scripted social exchanges that are repeated many times with only slight variation (Bretherton 1985). From these experiences with peers, the child internalizes a set of fundamental social expectations about the behavioural dispositions of the partner (Bowlby 1969/1982). These expectations form the basis for the development of an internal working model of relationships. Thus, through repeated experiences of social and social pretend play with a particular peer, a child forms an internal representation of a relationship with a playmate.

Some playmate relationships evolve into friendships. It is important to note that the child's representation of the partner comprises cognitions and affect derived from both the structure and the content of social experiences with that partner. Children who engage in repeated and complex interactions with a given playmate are likely to represent the partner as a friend. Furthermore, the content of interactions is likely to influence the quality of the resulting relationship.

Because settings for peer interaction contain individuals, dyads (child–caregiver; peer friendships and playmates), and at least one peer group, the interactions between children and caregivers and among peers, as well as the tone the caregivers set for the entire group all contribute to the social and emotional climate of the classroom or programme. Imagine a classroom setting in which most of the interactions were harmonious and respectful, in which children and adults worked together on projects, in which a child who was distressed or frustrated was comforted and helped, and in which laughter and other expressions of positive affect predominated. Contrast this with a classroom setting in which children were ridiculed for being different, talked to and touched in a harsh rejecting manner, competed rather than helped each other, and the general tone included mistrust and anger. We can imagine that the social development of children would take different paths in these two extremes. Because encounters with peers become experiences of 'living' within a group for the child, it is impossible to understand the social development of a child as isolated from the group.

Strategies for studying peer relations

Recognizing that the development of peer relations includes attending to individual child behaviours, to dyadic interactions and relationship quality, and to peer groups necessitates particular methodological strategies. Descriptions of children's socialization experiences must be at each level, individual, dyad and group. In order to fully understand the complexity of peer interaction within peer groups, interactions between levels of analysis (individual, dyad, group) must be considered. For example, a shy child may find engaging with peers more difficult in a hostile versus a harmonious classroom climate (Gazelle 2006). And having one peer who speaks your home language is a different experience from having your home language spoken by the entire group (Howes and Lee 2007; Howes *et al.* 2009). Analysis strategies must include attention to how individuals and dyads are nested within peer groups, to how groups are nested within settings, and to how settings are nested within and across cultural communities. Fortunately, advances in hierarchical linear modelling have made these multilevel analyses possible.

Most if not all of the research in this area requires time-consuming observing and interviewing within the programmes. Although there are valid and reliable measures of general setting characteristics, e.g. the Early Childhood Environmental Rating Scales (Harms *et al.* 1998) and the CLASS (Pianta *et al.* 2004), more targeted observational strategies usually require a time-sampling procedure, e.g. The Peer Play Scale (Howes and Matheson 1992). Inclusion of measures of the cultural community requires intensive open-ended interviews with adults by interviewers who are culturally as well as linguistically bilingual (Howes *et al.* 2007).

Beyond observing and describing peer encounters, careful observation and inference is necessary to interpret children's social behaviours, interactions and relationships. For example, when a two-year-old starts to join two other children playing in a water table the observer must attend carefully to body language, eye gaze and the affect of all three children to determine if the reason she quickly left was because the other children excluded her from play, a peer accidentally splashed her and she doesn't like being wet, or that she left because she was distracted by a child riding by on a bike. Children who are this young are very limited in their ability to reflect and to self-report on their own perceptions of interactions and relationships. Training and establishing reliability on observational coding schemes is extremely important in this area of research. By age three, children begin to reliably report on their social relationships with peers using sociometric methodology and their social and emotion regulation skills can be individually assessed (Raver 2004; Rubin *et al.* 2006).

If children and caregivers come from diverse cultural communities and particularly if the differences are mirrored by dominant/minority culture discrimination and racism, the children may fare better when there are caregivers who share the children's cultural communities (Baker *et al.* 1997; Howes and Ritchie 2002; Johnson *et al.* 2003). In one of our recent studies in very diverse low-income childcare settings in a city marked by heightened racial and ethnic conflict, we found that children who had conflictual interactions with teachers different from them in racial/ethnic heritage as they entered childcare had not achieved positive relationships with these teachers even after six months in the classroom (Howes and Shivers 2006). If we assume that having a positive teacher–child relationship is used as a secure base in forming relationships and developing play with peers is important, then these findings are disturbing.

In working with the construct of cultural community it is important to recognize that each individual can and most likely does participate in more than one cultural community (Rogoff 2003). While the participants, teachers and children in any given classroom come from several or only one home cultural community, by engaging with others within the classroom, they participate in a classroom cultural community. So teachers and children simultaneously participate in both cultural communities. Classrooms have common everyday practices. Where do you start your day? Sitting in your place on the rug for morning circle or having breakfast with a favourite caregiver, your brother and your cousin? If you disrupt the morning circle, do you lose minutes from outside play time, have to sit on a caregiver's lap or go to the time-out chair? Can you say 'you can't play' and to whom?

Feeling safe enough to enter into the world of peers

Working within an attachment perspective we assume that classroom cultural communities differ in children's feeling of trust and safety within the classroom (Howes and Ritchie 2002). Therefore in integrating a cultural communities perspective with an attachment perspective it is important to examine common everyday practices that help children feel sufficiently safe to explore the world of peer relations. We have identified four types of everyday classroom practices that help or hinder children from feeling safe enough to engage with peers. These are attachment relationships with caregivers; how teachers help children as they join the peer group; the social and emotional climate of the classroom; and the time to play.

Relationships with caregivers

Children with more secure attachments to caregivers are concurrently and longitudinally more socially competent with peers even when controlling for parental attachment quality (Howes 1999; Mitchell-Copeland *et al.* 1997; Pianta *et al.* 2002). We sometimes incorrectly assume that children who form more secure relationships with teachers are more competent with peers because a positive relationship is generalized or that sociable children form good relationships with all people. Working within attachment theory we assume that children who form secure teacher–child relationships have more competent peer relations because they use the teacher as a secure base. When a child trusts a caregiving adult to be positive, loving and warm then that child can use the adult as a base for exploration and mastery (Grossman *et al.* 1999).

Mastering peer relationships, particularly mastering competent cooperative play with peers, is easier when the child can explore and experiment with peers while making forays back to a trusted adult. If children feel valued and supported by a teacher, then they can try out what happens if they, for example, invite a potential friend to play, pretend to be a scary monster or stand their ground in the face of bullying. If children do not trust the teacher to value and support them, then it is all too easy to pick a fight, refuse to let someone play or hide from a bully.

Entering the peer group

Having adults as secure bases for exploring the peer group takes on added importance when children enter new peer groups. When children are new to peer groups they neither know the games nor the players, and thus may be at risk of exclusion from or withdrawing from already formed play groups (Feldbaum *et al.* 1980; Fox and Field 1989). Children who are excluded or who anxiously withdraw from peers miss opportunities to play with others and to develop social interaction and relationships skills with peers. So the time period when children enter new (to them) classrooms becomes an important stage-setting time for the development of peer relations. In early studies of children entering preschool (Feldbaum *et al.* 1980; Fox and Field 1989) children appeared to rely on adults during the transition to preschool. Typically children would spend most of the first two weeks in a new setting close to the adults and then begin playing with peers. Children who enter new classroom settings are from the first day assessing whom, among the adults in the setting, can be trusted. In one small-scale intensive study, children who successfully made attachment bids to new teachers in the first few days within a new classroom were assessed as having positive attachments with these teachers two months later (Howes and Oldham 2001). Being successful meant that the child asked for comfort and the teacher responded in a sensitive manner.

The story is different, from this attachment perspective, for children with previous maladaptive relationship histories. These children, who have not had experiences with trusting adults and secure base behaviours, are less likely to look for adults who can be trusted and more likely to antagonize teachers and peers as they enter the classroom (Howes and Ritchie 2002). The entry period is extremely important for these children. Encountering an adult who behaves in a warm and trustworthy manner can help such a child begin relationships with these new peers in a more positive manner (Howes and Ritchie 2002).

Social–emotional climate created for playing with peers

The social–emotional climate of the classroom is the third area where everyday practices within the classroom can enhance or impede the development of competent relationships with peers. Classrooms that score high on the measure of social–emotional climate are pleasant places where there are conversations, spontaneous laughter and enjoyment expressed as children and teachers engage in various activities and interactions. Teachers are warm and sensitive to all of the children; they are emotionally and physically involved with the children's activities and they are rarely intrusive, angry or annoyed. In these classrooms there are clear, but flexible, rules and expectations for classroom routines. Children tend to follow these rules so that teachers rarely have to employ control techniques. In contrast, classrooms with negative climates are characteristically filled with relational as well as physical aggression among children and hostile conflictual interactions between children and teachers. Children in these classrooms have few options for activities. Interactions and activities are adult driven and most often based on behavioural management of out-of-control children.

A positive emotional climate appears to facilitate peer-relationship development by providing rules for engagement that promote prosocial rather than hostile peer interactions. Children who experience positive emotional climates as three-year olds are also likely to have positive peer relationships as second or third graders (ECCRN 2008). If it is difficult for young children to construct play sequences when they are just developing the capacity to do so, it is even more difficult to do so when they are interrupted by conflict occurring around them. Positive social–emotional climates also can facilitate positive peer relationships in newly formed peer groups. When social–emotional climates are negative and hostile, children are challenged to create relationships and complex play (Howes *et al.* 2009).

Time and permission to play

Creating peer play requires teachers to create an environment that values play. Children need physical space to play, materials that encourage pretend (Sutterby and Frost 2006) and teachers who do not re-direct them from playing back to work. When teachers are pressured and expected to teach pre-academic content, early shared understandings about the importance of time, materials and spaces for enhancing peer play seem to fade into the background. In our own work we have seen the amount of time children engage in complex pretend play decrease over the 20 years we have been observing in local programmes (Howes and Wishard 2004). This decrease is consistent with anecdotal reports that programmes are providing relatively little unstructured time for children to play.

Closing thoughts

For most children, social interactions and relationships with adults and peers outside of their families occur within a peer group. Understanding the development of peer relations within context requires a theoretical framework that integrates theories of development with theories of development within context, and with theories of cultural community. It also requires attention to individuals, dyads, peer and classroom groupings, and to cultural communities. For many children encountering peers also involves encountering interactive styles and practices of engaging with others that are different than those they experience at home. These can be challenging experiences for young children who are just beginning to develop social skills and relationships. For research, and for the children, it is important to focus on the social and emotional climate of the programme.

Point for reflection and discussion

Howes points to the importance of the emotional climate of the setting in order for children to successfully enter peer groups and establish and maintain relationships. What can adult caregivers do to create a positive emotional climate? What might the role of humour be in the creation of emotional climate?

Note

1 Carollee Howes' work and that of her colleagues at the University of California at Los Angeles (UCLA) has centred on children's development of social relationships within families and child-care programmes. Los Angeles is the host location for the largest immigrant group in the United States, Mexican origin families, primarily from impoverished rural areas. It is also an international urban centre, which is diverse in social class, ethnicity and home language.

Bibliography

Baker, J.A., Terry, T., Bridger, R. and Winsor, A. (1997) 'Schools as caring communities: a relational approach to school reform'. *School Psychological Review*, 26: 586–602.

Bowlby, J. (1969/1982) *Attachment and Loss*. Volume 1: Attachment. London: Hogarth Press.

Bretherton, I. (1985) 'Attachment theory: retrospect and prospect'. *Monographs of the Society for Research in Child Development*, 50: 3–35.

Derman-Sparks, L. and the ABC Task Force (1989) *Anti-bias Curriculum: Tools for Empowering Young Children*. Washington, D.C.: National Association for the Education of Young Children.

Dunn, J. (2004) *Children's Friendships*. Malden, M.A.: Blackwell.

ECCRN, N. (2008) 'Social competence with peers in third grade: associations with earlier peer experiences in child care'. *Social Development,* 17: 419–54.

Feldbaum, C., Christenson, T. and O'Neal, E. (1980) 'An observational study of the assimilation of the newcomer to the preschool'. *Child Development,* 51: 497–507.

Fox, N.A. and Field, T.M. (1989) 'Individual differences in preschool entry behavior'. *Journal of Applied Developmental Psychology,* 10: 527–40.

Gazelle, H. (2006) 'Class climate moderates peer relations and emotional adjustment in children with an early history of anxious solitude: a child X environment model'. *Developmental Psychology,* 43: 1179–92.

Grossman, K.E., Grossman, K. and Zimmerman, P. (1999) 'A wider view of attachment and exploration: stability and change during the years of immaturity'. In J. Cassidy and P. Shaver (eds) *Handbook of Attachment: Theory Research and Clinical Implication*. New York City: Guilford, pp. 760–86.

Harms, T., Clifford, R.M. and Cryer, D. (1998) *Early Childhood Environment Rating Scale: Revised Edition*. New York: Teachers College Press.

Howes, C. (2009) *Culture and Child Development in Early Childhood Education: Practices, Activities, Interactions and Relationships*. Teachers College Press.

——(1999) 'Attachment relationships in the context of multiple caregivers'. In J. Cassidy and P.R. Shaver (eds) *Handbook of Attachment Theory and Research*. New York: Gilford, pp. 671–87

——(2008) 'Peer relationships in early childhood: friendship'. In K. Rubin, W. Bukowski and B. Laursen (eds) *Handbook of Peer Interaction, Relationships, and Groups*. Guilford.

Howes, C. and Lee, L. (2007) 'If you are not like me, can we play? Peer groups in preschool'. In B. Spodek and O. Saracho (eds) *Contemporary Perspectives on Research in Social Learning in Early Childhood Education*. Durham, N.C.: Information Age Publishing.

Howes, C. and Matheson, C.C. (1992) 'Sequences in the development of competent play with peers: social and social pretend play'. *Developmental Psychology*, 28: 961–74.

Howes, C. and Oldham, E. (2001) 'Processes in the formation of attachment relationships with new caregivers'. In A. Goncu and E. Klein (eds) *Children in Play, Story and School*. New York: Greenwood.

Howes, C. and Ritchie, S. (2002) *A Matter of Trust: Connecting Teachers and Learners in the Early Childhood Classroom*. New York: Teachers College Press.

Howes, C., Sanders, K. and Lee, L. (2009) 'Entering a new peer group in ethnically and linguistically diverse child care classrooms'. *Social Development*, 17(4): 922–40.

Howes, C. and Shivers, E.M. (2006) 'New child-caregiver attachment relationships: entering child care when the caregiver is and is not an ethnic match'. *Social Development*, 15: 343–60.

Howes, C. and Spieker, S. (2008) 'Attachment relationships in the context of multiple caregivers'. In J. Cassidy and P.R. Shaver (eds) *Handbook of Attachment Theory and Research, second edition*. New York City: Guilford Publications.

Howes, C. and Wishard, A. G. (2004) 'Revisiting sharing meaning: looking through the lens of culture and linking shared pretend play through proto narrative development to emergent literacy'. In E. Zigler, D.G. Singer and S.J. Bishop-Josef (eds) *Children's Play: The Roots of Literacy*. Washington, D.C.: Zero to Three, pp. 143–58.

Howes, C., Wishard Guerra, A.G. and Zucker, E. (2007) 'Cultural communities and parenting in Mexican-heritage families'. *Parenting:Science and Practice*, 7: 1–36.

Huijbregts, S.K., Leseman, P.P.M. and Tavecchio, L.W. (2008) 'Cultural diversity in center-based childcare: childrearing beliefs of professional caregivers from different cultural communities in the Netherlands'. *Early Childhood Research Quarterly*, 23: 233–45.

Johnson, D.J., Jaeger, E., Randolph, S.M., Cauce, A.M., Ward, J. and Eccrn, N. (2003) 'Studying the effects of early child care experiences on the development of children of color in the United States: towards a more inclusive research agenda'. *Child Development*, 74: 1227–44.

Justice, L., Cottone, E.A., Mashburn, A. and Rimm-Kaufman, S.E. (2008) 'Relationships between teachers and preschoolers who are at risk: contributions of children's language skills, temperamentally based attributes, and gender'. *Early Education and Development*, 19: 600–22.

Lubeck, S. (1996). 'Deconstructing "child development knowledge" and "teacher preparation"'. *Early Childhood Research Quarterly*, 11: 147–67.

Mitchell-Copeland, J., Denham, S. and DeMulder, E. (1997) 'Q-Sort assessment of child–teacher attachment relationships and social competence in the preschool'. *Early Education and Development*, 8: 27–39.

Pianta, R.C., Hamre, B. and Stuhlman, M. (eds) (2002) *Relationships between Teachers and Children*, Vol. 7. New York: Wiley.

Pianta, R.C., LaParo, K.M. and Hamre, B. (2004) *Classroom Assessment Scoring System*. University of Virginia.

Raver, C.C. (2004) 'Placing emotional self-regulation in sociocultural and socioeconomic contexts'. *Child Development*, 75: 346–53.

Rogoff, B. (2003) *The Cultural Nature of Human Development.* New York: Oxford University Press.

Rubin, K.H., Bukowski, W. and Parker, J. (2006) 'Peer interactions, relationships, and groups'. In N. Eisenberg, W. Damon and R. Lerner (eds) *Handbook of Child Psychology: Vol. 3, Social, Emotional, and Personality Development.* Hoboken, N.J.: John Wiley & Sons, pp. 571–645.

Spinrad, T.L., Eisenberg, N., Harris, E., Hanish, L., Fabes, R.A. *et al.* (2004) 'The relation of children's everyday nonsocial peer play behavior to their emotionality, regulation and social functioning'. *Developmental Psychology,* 40: 67–80.

Sutterby, J.A. and Frost, J. (2006) 'Creating play environments for early childhood: Indoors and out'. In B. Spodek and O. Saracho (eds) *Handbook of Research on the Education of Young Children.* Mahwah, N.J.: Lawrence Erlbaum & Associates, pp. 305–22.

Wishard, A., Shivers, E., Howes, C. and Ritchie, S. (2003) 'Child care program and teacher practices: associations with quality and children's experiences'. *Early Childhood Research Quarterly,* 18: 65–103.

Chapter 3

Children's and parents' perspectives on play and friendships

Margaret Kernan[1]

Attending to playfulness in peer relations in pedagogy

Both parents and children recognize that early childhood education and care settings and schools are an important source of playmates and friends and are influential in children's overall welfare. However, it is arguable as to whether this is taken into account in the elaboration of curricula and in the organization of spaces and times in these settings. My aim in this chapter is to give voice to both children's and parents' perspectives regarding peers, playmates and friendships. In many ways, this focus reflects the wave of interest in accessing children's perspectives on their experiences, which has been a central theme of discussion in childhood sociology and the broader social studies of childhood in the present decade (Clark, Kjørholt and Moss 2005; Mayall 2002). The notion of children's perspectives or children's voice has come to mean how adults and society try to understand children's lives, as well as how children themselves experience and describe their lives (Brostrom 2006). Within early childhood education and care specifically, this has been incorporated into pedagogical approaches where both adults and children have 'a say' and attention is paid to creating practices that are in tune with children's way of thinking, communicating and being (Bae 2009; Edwards *et al.* 1998; Jans 2004; OECD 2006).

It is in this pedagogical 'space' that play, playfulness and children's peer relationships have an important role. Firstly, play and playful actions have a contribution to make to the rise and maintenance of children's connectedness and togetherness (Hännikäinen 2001), and consequently feelings of belonging to a peer culture within children's centres or schools. Secondly, 'playful' features of young children's communication and being also serve as balance or counterpoint to the oftentimes rigidity of adult's agendas in educational and care provision, evident in institutional routines and regulations, or in the emphasis on meeting academic learning goals (see also Chapter 5 of this volume for a further discussion on this issue).

The chapter draws on a number of studies that have explored girls' and boys' perspectives on and experiences of their social lives. In the first section, I briefly discuss the position or status of peer relations in early childhood education and care settings. Parents' views on their children's peer relationships provide the focus for the following section. Then I discuss the strategies children employ to maintain togetherness in peer relations, as well as their experience of inclusion and exclusion. In these two sections I draw particularly on studies conducted in early childhood education and care and school settings in Ireland. In the final section of the chapter, strategies adults can employ to ensure that all children can achieve a positive sense of self and feeling of belonging in peer relations are discussed.

Play and peer relationships in curricula for early childhood education and care

Much of the interest in play and peer relationships in early childhood education and care stems from the identified potential of play, particularly joint peer play and socio-dramatic or pretend play, for children to learn and develop the social skills necessary to become socially competent (Garvey 1977; Giffin 1984; Vygotsky 1978). This is viewed as necessary for the 'here and now' daily social life of children attending group settings, and learning the social skills, self-regulation and control that are deemed necessary for life as a school pupil.

As illustrated in other chapters in this volume, the place of play and peer relations in curricula for early education and care are influenced by a range of factors including historical and cultural traditions and values, dominant political discourses, the age of children involved and the main goals of setting. Singer and de Haan (Chapter 8 this volume) link the low priority afforded to peer friendships of children aged zero to four years in childcare settings in the Netherlands to the main goal of these settings: care on the specific days that the part-time working parents are not available at home. Care during working hours of the parents is much more important than stability in group composition. In contrast, Corsaro and Molinari (2008) describe how the organization of both pre-school and primary education in Italy works to built up a community among children, teachers and parents. They ensure stability in peer groups, i.e. keeping groups of children together, where activities such as playing, eating and working together are viewed as important as individual academic tasks.

In many settings, particularly in the transition to more formal primary school, features of children's joint play such as freedom, spontaneity, exuberance, fun and ownership tend to be marginalized to the outdoor break, often viewed as the non-teaching, or 'down tools' time by adults, where a distinction is made between the outdoors as the arena for non-serious play or running about with friends, recreation, or 'letting off steam' and indoors, as the arena for serious work and learning (quiet and sitting down) (Evans and Pellegrini 1997; Kernan and Devine 2009; Pellegrini 2005). Adults, parents and teachers, have a great impact on children's opportunities to develop friendships. Let us examine the parents' perspectives regarding their children's peer relationships.

Significance of peer relationships and friendships to children – what do parents say?

During the 1990s the findings of the cross-national IEA Pre-primary Project indicated remarkable consistency between early years practitioners and parents in the 15 participating countries[2] in the priority afforded social skills with peers as among the *most important skills* for young children to develop in early childhood education and care between ages three to five (Weikart 1999).

The importance of their children being happy and having friends to play with was a theme in parents' narratives in a multidimensional study into the experiences of the outdoors in four settings in a large urban centre in Ireland (Kernan and Devine 2009). These settings, which reflected the diversity of early childhood education and care provision in Ireland, were a day nursery, workplace crèche, a community pre-school playgroup and a reception class of a primary school.[3] At the core of the research was the exploration of the outdoor experiences of eight focal children aged between one and five years. Fieldwork incorporated a 'day in the life diary' completed by parents and semi-structured interviews with parents with shared viewing of photographs. A key rationale in incorporating a 'day in the life perspective' (Warming and Kampmann 2007) was to capture the realities of young children's everyday lives negotiated between home settings and the neighbourhood spaces 'in-between'.

The following is an excerpt from the study where Ella's (aged four years and one month) mother, Alison, describes her priorities for Ella in the community playgroup she attends four mornings a week:

> Because Ella is their only child, Alison and Brian [her parents] were keen that she get used to group life with other children. Brian is from a very large family, and is particularly concerned about how being an only child might affect Ella:
>
> 'I was looking for somewhere she could play, get used to other children, get used to getting a few knocks before she started school' …
>
> When she goes into the playgroup room, Ella always goes first to the sand tray at the back of the room. Alison waits with her until she has settled. She feels that Ella has struggled to make friends in the group because the majority of the 22 children [in the group] were there the previous year:
>
> 'I found that when Ella started these are the bigger kids, they're all nearly a year older … and I found that they wouldn't sort of let her in' …
>
> As Alison views the photographs that I have taken of Ella at various points during that morning in playgroup she remarks:
>
> 'It's nice to see them happy, because you don't know when you leave sometimes whether … It's great to see that you are looking at your child there and she's happy. That would be my main thing, that she would be happy'.
>
> (Kernan 2006)

Energy and physical activity in play with and without peers are recurring themes in the narrative of Nuala when describing her son Jack's (aged four years and eleven months) day, half of which is spent in Stepside Infant School. Here she describes meeting Jack at the end of a school day:

> He is out of the school like a bullet, and he always runs down the hill ... I think its because he's free from school – it's the freedom. Often he is with Leo or Cormac two of his friends because they walk that way too. They run across the parking area and wait for Nuala at the bottom of the steps that lead up to the pathway along the main road. He then climbs over the wall and runs through the gardens of three small houses side by side. He loves doing that.

There are no children living close by on the street where Jack lives, so playing with friends at home is something that has to be organized. On the other hand, weekend and holiday time in the outdoor public space in front of his grandmother's home away from the city provided opportunities for informal, unplanned-for play outdoors for Jack in the company of other children. This is described by Nuala as follows:

> There is a big green in front of her house, and there are loads of children out playing there. Jack has more freedom outdoors there. There's a gate between the green and the main road. We know he's safe because we can see him from the house.

Nuala's narratives intermingle her recognition of the importance of freedom and playing with peers for Jack with a concern for his safety outdoors – in particular her fear that someone would abduct him (Kernan 2006). Different kinds of fears are expressed by the parents interviewed by Pinkster (2009) in a study that investigated the interaction between neighborhood and family circumstances and peer relationships in a low-income, culturally heterogeneous urban neighbourhood in the Netherlands. Here, parents worried both that their children might become victims of crime, and that their children would be corrupted through acquiring the 'wrong' friends on the street and in school. This concern was present from age four, which in common with the situation in Ireland, represents the primary school starting age for most children in the Netherlands. Pinkster writes, 'When parents talk about the composition of the school population of local schools, their main concern is the school as a source of potential playmates rather than the negative consequences of a minority school composition for their child's cognitive development' (Pinkster, 2009: 329). A further finding of this study was that parents who were slightly better educated were more likely to choose a non-neighbourhood school. They were also more likely to distance themselves from other residents and to select their children's friends. Pinkster (2009) also noted that monitoring children's peer relationships was particularly challenging for single parents. Being home to structure their children's lives and protect them from unwanted neighbourbood influences was an important reason for some single mothers interviewed in this study to stay on welfare rather than to try and find a job.

In both of these studies it becomes apparent that parents are aware of the importance of peer friendships for their children. We are also made aware of parents' anxieties around perceived risks and opportunities in children's peer friendships and the degree to which they can be monitored by parents. What about children's perspectives?

The importance of togetherness with friends for children

The importance of peers to children is consistently present in the narratives of children in early and middle childhood, irrespective of cultural background (Ansell 2005) and social class (Sutton *et al.* 2007). It is also often at the top of young children's agenda when they are asked about what is important to them in their daily lives at pre-school (Sheridan and Pramling Samuelsson 2001; Torstenson-Ed 2007), school (Devine 2003; Mayall 2002) or after-school services (Petrie *et al.* 2000). Being part of the group is very important for most children. A key finding of a study of migrant children's experiences of living in Ireland was that having friends and making connections with others was more important to them than emphasizing their national and ethnic differences (Ní Laoire, Bushin, Carpena-Méndez and White 2009). In particular, missing old friends in their countries of origin, maintaining contact with these friends and making new friends were viewed by the 190 children aged 3–18 who were interviewed as part of this study, as being extremely important.

Recognizing the importance of friendships to children and how they can be best supported in their social lives, a number of researchers have explored the verbal and non-verbal strategies young children employ to maintain togetherness, sustain friendships and repair relations after conflicts. Common features highlighted in the studies of Dunn (1993), Hännikäinen (2001), de Haan and Singer (2001, Chapter 8 this volume), and Corsaro (2005) include the use of humour; joking and playing with language and exaggeration; using 'rude' words and laughter. Other verbal strategies utilized are 'we' talk, explicit reference to sameness; enthusiastic greetings, questioning features of the other, and compliments. Spontaneity and flexibility have also been identified as important in friendship formation: 'Children who are joyous, energetic and spontaneous gather friends around them. They send out positive messages to others and receive positive affirmation in return' (Murray, 2008).

Sometimes strategies employed by children are physical. As noted by Paley (2004), 'when nothing more dramatic came to mind, children maintained contact by grabbing at one another … anything to keep the connections alive' (2004: 18). Physically active play, high-energy behaviours and exaggerated movements such as running, chasing, fleeing or wrestling (Maccoby 1998) have also been identified as 'children's way of feeling connected' (Perry, 2001: 12). As children move from early childhood to middle childhood years, sharing common interests, solidarity and supportiveness assume importance in peer relations and are valued by children in their friendships (Mayall 2002). 'Being funny' was an additional trait in friends that was valued by the seven- to eleven-year-old children interviewed by Devine (2003) regarding their experiences of primary school in Ireland.

Thus, it becomes clear that children are motivated to be affiliated. Their primary aim is to connect with others, to fit in and be part of the group, to understand and be understood (Brennan 2008). Observations and interviews with three-, four- and five-year-old children regarding their experiences outdoors in early childhood education and care and school settings in the study referred to earlier, suggested that the need for affiliation with their (same-sex) peers was hugely important to the children (Kernan 2010). In the Willow Day Nursery, the freedom of the outdoors provided greater scope for collaborative play and peer affiliation to develop between boys outdoors than indoors, where joint interests involved large movements, locomotion, transporting and running, all of which were more acceptable to adults outdoors than indoors. Indoors and outdoors, boys and girls were often observed to create small hiding spaces to be in pairs away from the group. The top of a slide was sometimes colonized by two of the older girls for this purpose.

From the perspectives of both the children and practitioners interviewed in Stepside Infant School, indoors in the classroom appeared principally to be the domain of work that was directed by the adult, and outdoors, the domain of play that was directed by the children, albeit with certain limits and boundaries set by adults. When children were asked about the favourite place in school, all were unequivocal in their choice of the outdoor playground. This did not necessarily mean that the outdoor time and space was unproblematic for the children. Rejection and exclusion by peers were also part of children's outdoor play experiences. Not surprisingly, themes of power and control, inclusion and exclusion feature in prominent studies of children's play with peers such as those conducted by Corsaro (2005), Dunn (1985) and Paley (1992). The following excerpts from an ethnographic and interpretative study of children's participation in socio-dramatic play in another setting in Ireland – a suburban preschool playgroup, which was conducted by Brennan (2008), provide a useful lens to understanding the role these play in peer relationships.

Inclusion and exclusion in play and peer relationships

The study took place over one school year and involved 22 children ranging in age from two years and eight months to four years and nine months. Brennan observed the children's socio-dramatic play during indoor 'free play' sessions using video. Free play sessions typically lasted for 90 minutes. Using a small handheld camera, the researcher followed children's play as unobtrusively as possible. In total over 470 play episodes were documented, which brought the reader into the world of systems, rules, relationships and agendas that children enact in their play. In the following excerpt from the study, Brennan reflects on the power distribution and negotiation involved when children were playing in groups of three.

> Threesomes often present problems among the more socially aware girls and boys in this group, because power distribution and negotiation is more challenging when there are combination options. Resistance to others' control and feelings of insecurity are prevalent among them. Sarah struggles for recognition when she plays with Greg and Mairéad. Judy struggles in the trio with Sarah and Amy. Mairéad resents any bonding between Sarah and Judy, and Amy also feels threatened when Sarah and Judy lead the game [...] Yet threesomes almost inevitably

> involve conflict and these moments of raised consciousness sometimes appear emotionally painful and critical in identity formation. On the positive side, the children undoubtedly carry with them the benefits of resolved relationship problems and happy play encounters. In their moments of conflict, however, I also see children's insecurities and hurt and I wonder about the narrative that they construct. They can be stories of rejection or of problem solution. I am conscious that how children narrate and structure these experiences to themselves and others is of critical importance to their construction of identity.
>
> (Brennan, 2008: 240–1)

Throughout all the data in this study, the emotional child is to the fore. In order to participate in socio-dramatic play, Brennan concludes, children need to be able to communicate and connect at action, verbal and emotional levels in culturally appropriate ways and to engage with the growing complexity of shared meanings and relationships and membership criteria within the group. Not all of the children were successful in entering the subgroups. Brennan writes: 'One child repeatedly broke the rules of play and consequently was repeatedly expelled by the players. Another child lacked connective social skills and following many experiences of failure largely gave up trying. Another was often rejected because she appeared controlling and distrustful' (Brennan, 2008: 175). Specific adult support and intervention may have supported these children in their efforts to build relationships and be accepted in the group.

Strategies of teachers and parents to support playing with friends

Adults can employ several strategies in creating conditions that support children in forming friendship relations. Firstly, it is important to reiterate the importance of creating environments where children feel safe and secure to broaden their social circle. Other chapters in this volume have emphasized the importance of secure relationships with familiar adults and this is reiterated here. Secondly, it is also important for adults to model and provide opportunities for children to practice the skills and strategies of successful friends and players referred to earlier in this chapter such as empathy, helpfulness, interest in others, establishing common ground and coordinating contributions. Thirdly, it is important to keep in mind that the organization of the physical space indoors and outdoors has a bearing on children's experiences of peer relationships.

The term 'unobtrusive player' has been used to describe a role whereby the adult can enrich peer play, extend its duration, promote social competence and at the same time gain insight into the concerns and interests of the children. This can include, as in Perry's framework (2001), organizing the ecology of the space in diverse areas that are predictable, familiar and capitalize on children's interests; observing children's interactions with others noting anything that confuses or obstructs the progress of peer play; actively promoting peer play by setting up activities that involve face-to-face play; avoiding overcrowding and noticing children who are disengaged and uninvolved with either materials or playmates. Brennan (2008) suggests that having identified the children who need additional support, adults can avail themselves of opportunities to build each child's identity as someone who contributes, who has good ideas and who plays with other children. Partnering competent and less competent children together, and teaching conflict resolution skills are also recommended (see also Chapter 9 and 10 this volume).

As children get older and make the transition to more formalized school settings with clearly delineated recreation times and spaces, attention also needs be paid to issues of overcrowding and the design of play spaces. Mayall (2002) for example notes that bullying and accidents are less likely to occur in spacious play areas, where children can spread out. Differences in girls' and boys' strategies in maintaining peer relationships should also be taken into account in the design of the outdoor space. A balance between spaces for manufactured play equipment, green areas with vegetation and pathways, which are conducive to social interaction in a non-competitive context, with more open play fields or areas for team games such as football is advisable (Dyment *et al.* 2009).

Finally, for both younger and older children, it is important to note the significance of two children from the same group or class, meeting to play together outside school time. This is often viewed by children as an important marker of friendship within a group. In two of the studies discussed in this chapter (Kernan and Devine 2009 and Brennan 2008) 'play visits' at children's homes were significant milestones in children's friendship development. Practitioners and parents can work together in supporting younger children in seeking out friends, by sharing information with each other regarding emerging friendships between children. This may be particularly important in a situation where a child struggles to belong to a class community. A visit to a classmate's home to play may be an important catalyst in the process of developing a friendship, a common-ground and a sense of belonging.

Concluding comments

In many communities the opportunities for children for spontaneous interaction and play with peers at home and outdoors in the neighbourhood are diminishing. This is due to factors such as the dominance of car traffic, the reduced availability of other children to play with and parents' and children's concerns about children's safety outdoors. Consequently, organized group settings such as early childhood education and care centres and schools have become important sites for children to find playmates and participate in peer culture. Parents and children are aware of this. It is vital that, in their planning, practitioners and policymakers also take into account the importance of peer relations and friendships for children's welfare in group settings. In brief, children need time and physical and social environments where they feel safe and secure to forge connections with peers and develop and practise the skills necessary to establish and maintain friendships. They also need adults who are prepared to listen to them, and who are skilled at observing the progress of play and friendship and take action to support children who are struggling in their peer relationships.

Finally, it is in the best interests of children and communities if parents, early childhood education and care settings, and neighbourhoods work together to improve young children's access to time and space for social interaction with peers.

Acknowledgements

Acknowledgements are due to Carmel Brennan for permission to cite material from her thesis (Brennan 2008).

Point for reflection and discussion

The importance to children of feeling connected to others and having friends to play with are highlighted in this chapter. How do children form and maintain friendships? What can practitioners do to help children who struggle to be part of the group? How can early childhood education and care settings, schools and neighbourhoods work together to improve children's access to spaces for social interaction with peers?

Notes

1 Margaret Kernan has worked as a practitioner, trainer and researcher in early childhood education and care and primary education in Ireland, England and the Netherlands. She situates her work within the interdisciplinary social studies of childhood and enjoys the challenge of cross-disciplinary research. A particular interest has been the role of play in children's lives at home, in care and educational settings and in the neighbourhood in urban settings. Margaret is currently a Senior Programme Manager in International Child Development Initiatives (ICDI), Leiden, the Netherlands.

2 IEA stands for International Association for the Evaluation of Educational Achievement. The IEA Preprimary Project was a large cross-national investigation into the years prior to children's entry into compulsory education. Participating countries were: Belgium, China, Finland, Greece, Hong Kong, Indonesia, Ireland, Italy, Nigeria, Poland, Romania, Slovenia, Spain, Thailand and the United States (Weikart, 1999).

3 Although children are not required by law to attend school until they have reached their sixth birthday in Ireland, virtually all five-year-olds and more than half of four-year-olds attend the junior infant classes (reception class) of primary school.

Bibliography

Ansell, N. (2005) *Children, Youth and Development*. London: Routledge.

Bae, B. (2009) 'Children's right to participate – challenges in everyday interactions'. *European Early Childhood Education Research Journal*, 17(3): 391–406.

Brennan, C. (2008) 'Partners in play: how children organise their participation in sociodramatic play'. Unpublished PhD thesis. Dublin Institute of Technology, Dublin.

Brostrom, S. (2006) 'Children's perspectives on their childhood experiences'. In J. Einarsdottir and J.T. Wagner (eds) *Nordic Childhoods and Early Education: Philosophy, Research, Policy and Practice in Denmark, Finland, Iceland, Norway and Sweden*. Greenwich, C.T.: Information Age.

Christensen, P. and James, A. (2000) 'Introduction'. In P. Christensen and A. James (eds) *Research with Children: Perspectives and Practices*. London: Falmer Press.

Corsaro, W.A. (2003) *We're Friends, Right? Inside Kids' Culture*. Washington, D.C.: Joseph Henry Press.

——(2005) *The Sociology of Childhood*, second edition. Thousand Oaks, C.A.: Pine Forge Press.

Corsaro, W. and Molinari, L. (2008) 'Policy and practice in Italian children's transition from preschool to elementary school'. *Research in Comparative and International Education*, 3(3): 250–65.

Clark, A., Kjørholt, A.T. and Moss, P. (eds.) (2005) *Beyond Listening: Children's Perspectives on Early Childhood Services*. Bristol: Policy Press.

Devine, D. (2003) *Children, Power and Schooling: How Childhood is Structured in the Primary School*. Stoke-on-Trent: Trentham Books.

Dunn, J. (1985) *Sisters and Brothers*. Cambridge, M.A.: Harvard University Press.

——(1993) *Young Children's Close Relationships: Beyond Attachment*. Newbury Park, C.A.: Sage.

——(2004) *Children's Friendships: The Beginnings of Intimacy*. Oxford: Blackwell.

Dyment, J.E., Bell, A.C. and Lucas, A.J. (2009) 'The relationship between school ground design and intensity of physical activity'. *Children's Geographies*, 7(3): 261–77.

Edwards, C., Gandini, L. and Forman, G. (1998) *The Hundred Languages of Children*. Greenwich, C.T.: Ablex.

Evans, J. and Pellegrini, A.D. (1997) 'Surplus energy theory: an enduring but inadequate justification for break time'. *Educational Review*, 48: 229–36.

Garvey, C. (1977) *Play*. Cambridge, M.A.: Harvard University Press.

Giffin, H. (1984) 'The coordination of meaning in the creation of shared make-believe reality'. In I. Bretherton (ed) *Symbolic Play: the Development of Social Understanding*. New York: Academic Press.

de Haan, D. and Singer, E. (2001) 'Young children's language of togetherness'. *International Journal of Early Years Education*, 9(2): 117–24.

Hännikäinen, M. (2001) 'Playful actions as a sign of togetherness in day care centres'. *International Journal of Early Years Education*, 9(2): 125–34.

Jans, M. (2004) 'Children as citizens: towards a contemporary notion of child participation'. *Childhood*, 11(1): 27–44.

Kernan, M. (2006) 'The place of the outdoors in constructions of a "good" childhood: an interdisciplinary study of outdoor provision in early childhood education in urban settings'. Unpublished PhD thesis. Dublin: University College Dublin.

Kernan, M. and Devine, D. (2009) 'Being confined within? Constructions of the good childhood and outdoor play in early childhood education and care settings in Ireland'. *Children & Society*, early view July 2009. doi 10.1111/j.1099-0860.2009.00249.x

Kernan, M. (2010) 'Outdoor affordances in early childhood education and care settings: adults' and children's perspectives'. *Children, Youth and Environments*, 20(1): 152–77.

Maccoby, E.E. (1998) *The Two Sexes: Growing Up Apart, Coming Together*. Cambridge, M.S.: Belknap and Harvard University.

Mayall, B. (2002) *Towards a Sociology for Childhood: Thinking from Children's Lives*. Buckingham: Open University Press.

Moss, P. and Petrie, P. (2002) *From Children's Services to Children's Spaces: Public Policy, Children and Childhood*. London: Routledge Falmer.

Murray, M. (2008) 'Encouraging a joyous approach'. *The Irish Times*, 2 February 2008.

Ní Laoire, C., Bushin, N., Carpena-Méndez, F. and White, A. (2009) *Tell Me About Yourself: Migrant Children's Experiences of Moving to and Living in Ireland*, Final Report of the Marie Curie Excellence Team Project Migrant Children: Children's and Young People's Experiences of Immigration and Integration in Irish Society. Cork: University College Cork. http://migration.ucc.ie/children/finalreport.html [accessed 11 November 2009].

OECD (2006) *Starting Strong II*. Paris: Organisation for Economic Co-operation and Development.
Paley, V.G. (1992) *You Can't Say You Can't Play*. Cambridge, M.A.: Harvard University Press.
——(2004) *A Child's Work: the Importance of Fantasy Play*. Chicago: University of Chicago Press.
Pellegrini, A.D. (2005) *Recess: its Role in Education and Development*. Mahwah, N.J.: Lawrence Erlbaum Associates.
Petrie, P., Egharevba, I., Oliver, C. and Poland, G. (2000) *Out-of-School Lives, Out-of-School Services*. London: Stationery Office.
Pinkster, F.M. (2009) 'Watch out for the neighborhood trap! A case study on parental perceptions of and strategies to counter risks for children in a disadvantaged neighbourhood'. *Children's Geographies*, 7(3): 323–38.
Perry, J.P. (2001) *Outdoor Play: Teaching Strategies with Young Children*. New York: Teachers College, Columbia University.
Sheridan, S. and Pramling Samuelsson, I. (2001) 'Children's conceptions of participation and influence in pre-school: a perspective on pedagogical quality'. *Contemporary Issues in Early Childhood*, 2: 169–94.
Sutton, L., Smith, L., Dearden, C. and Middleton, S. (2007) *A Child's Eye View of Social Difference*. York: Joseph Rowntree Foundation.
Torstenson-Ed, T. (2007) 'Children's life paths through preschool and school: letting youths talk about their own childhood – theoretical and methodological conclusions'. *Childhood*, 14, 47–66.
Vygotsky, L. (1978) *Mind in Society: the Development of Higher Psychological Processes*. Cambridge, M.A.: Harvard University Press.
Warming, H. and Kampmann, J. (2007) 'Children in command of time and space'. In H. Zeiher, D. Devine, A. Kjørholt, H. Strandell (eds) *Children's Times and Spaces: Changes in Welfare in an Intergenerational Perspective*. Odense: University Press of Southern Denmark.
Weikart, D. (1999) *What Should Young Children Learn? Teacher and Parent Views in 15 Countries, IEA Preprimary Project Phase 2*. Ypsilanti: High/Scope Press.

Chapter 4

Rethinking young children's rights for participation in diverse cultural contexts

Anne Trine Kjørholt[1]

Introduction

The United Nations Convention on the Rights of the Child (UNCRC) including the constructing of children as competent social actors with rights to be listened to and to have a say in matters that affect their lives, represents an important tool to improve children's well-being and everyday lives in different parts of the world. Global rights discourses have been increasingly powerful worldwide since the adoption of the UNCRC in 1989, both in policy as well as in research. Young children's rights, and research, policies and practices regarding early childhood are also part of these global discourses. Participation rights as specifically formulated in articles 12 and 13 in UNCRC have been described as revolutionary compared to rights in earlier children's rights declarations. Based on these participation rights, it has been argued that children are social actors, also having rights as citizens, and that this view represents a new perspective on children. This view is reflected in the comments of the Committee on the Rights of the Child in their responses to the individual country reports regarding the implementation of the UNCRC related to early childhood. The Committee on the Rights of the Child argues that:

> There has been a shift away from traditional beliefs that regard early childhood mainly as a period for the socialization of the immature human being towards mature adult status [...]. The Convention requires that children, including the very youngest children, be respected as persons in their own right. Young children should be recognized as active members of families, communities and societies, with their own concerns, interests and points of view.
>
> (UN Committee on the Rights of the Child 2006: 2–3)

It is interesting to note that the Committee refers to a change with regard to notions of young children and persuades the states to create a positive agenda for implementing rights in early childhood.

The rights in the UNCRC are anchored in the recognition of children as individuals and competent social subjects. This implies a process of *individualization* of children in the way that they are increasingly removed from being defined within the framework of the family and are instead connected to the state by being treated as individuals in their own right (Näsman 1994; Mortier 2002). Historically, human rights, including rights for children, have had a central place in the welfare policies in Nordic countries (Bartley 1998).

Studies of how young children's rights to participation are interpreted and practised within early childhood services in a Nordic context indicate that participation is linked to autonomy, self-determination and individual rights to freedom of choice. It has been argued that this is connected to a particular notion of what it means to be a human being, anchored in the ideal of the mature human being as autonomous, rational and capable of formulating his or her needs and interest. This notion of the human subject, which can be traced back to the tradition of Emmanuel Kant, has been criticized for representing a particularistic notion of the human being, overlooking the fact that human beings, whether they be adults or children, are dependent in the sense that they are constituted within a web of social relationships to others (Kjørholt 2005). Furthermore, this connection of agency to individual autonomy and self-determination is particularly problematic in many countries in the majority South, because it represents a break with 'traditional' practices and local notions of the human being seen as part of an extended family and communities in complex ways. In spite of a growing interest in the field in recent decades, there is still a lack of empirical studies of the implementation of UNCRC in different cultural contexts, as well as a lack of theorizing regarding what it means to give young children rights to participation within early childhood education and care. Friendship and social relationships to peers are important from an early age for children spending their everyday lives within early childhood education and care institutions. Ethnographic studies in early childhood education and care in different social cultural contexts reveal that toddlers and older children spend a lot of their time in meaning-making processes with children of their same age group. It has been argued that children participate in two cultures – with adults and with peers – and that there is a tendency to overlook the latter (Corsaro 2003). There is a need for rethinking young children's rights to participation, focusing on how autonomy and the need for connectedness are closely intertwined. Furthermore, it is important to gain insight into how connectedness and autonomy are expressed and practised in diverse cultural contexts, and how the variety of social meaning-making processes with peers are interconnected with social relationships to adults and the broader cultural context.

The aim of this chapter is to rethink young children's rights to participation in early childhood education and care. I will connect the discussion to studies of how children's rights to participation are implemented in a Nordic context, revealing how the global rights discourses on participation and 'the best interest of the child' are linked to 'national' and local constructions of an 'ideal' or 'proper' childhood. By questioning autonomy, individual choice and self-determination that seem to be core issues in the practices related to giving children a voice, I will discuss alternative ways of implementing participation rights, pointing to children's need for connectedness and belonging in diverse cultural contexts. An interrelated approach to rights is highlighted. In particular I will draw on perspectives elaborated in the book *Beyond Listening:*

Children's Perspectives on Early Childhood Services (Clark *et al.* 2005). The philosophy of listening, understood as an 'ethic of an encounter', represents a broad approach to participation and listening to children in early childhood education and care, far beyond the scope of human experiences limited only to autonomy, cognitive abilities and oral language. As part of this approach, in the final section of the chapter, I pay attention to how children, practitioners and parents can engage in reflexive practices related to interpretations of events, phenomena and 'lived lives' in everyday life, by using a variety of different methods.

Rights to participation – examples from a Nordic context

In Nordic countries, discourses on children as autonomous and competent claimers of rights have been particularly powerful (Brembeck *et al.* 2004; Gulløv 2003; Kampmann 2004; Kjørholt 2005). Since the UNCRC was ratified in Norway in 1991, discourses on children's rights to participation have been powerful in Norwegian children's policy related to school reform, political participation and local planning. The construction of children as competent social actors with rights to participate in and influence everyday life has been apparent in both policy and research since the late 1980s (James *et al.* 1998; Clark *et al.* 2005). However, it is not until recently that these discourses have spread to early childhood education and care. Today children's right to participation is included in the national Kindergarten Act (2006) as well as in the national curriculum, the so-called Framework Plan for the Content and Tasks of Kindergartens (2006).

The implementation of the different articles in the UNCRC is dependent on culturally based values and interpretation influenced by the context in which they are implemented. In that sense the practices in early childhood education and care to a certain extent reflect cultural and political norms. This in itself is not problematic; what is difficult, however, is the fact that these values are often taken for granted and not explicitly discussed. Pertinent questions to be addressed are: What does it mean to give young children rights to participation within early childhood education and care services, in Norway called *barnehager* – kindergarten?[2] How are children allowed to express their views, and in regard to what? The rights in the UNCRC are formulated as universal statements. However, these rights as well as the principle of 'the best interests of the child' are not neutral, but refer to standards with different meanings across cultures, and due to class, ethnicity, gender and so on. Philip Alston points out that, whereas a child's individuality and autonomy will be valued as being in line with the principle of the 'best interests of the child' in modern Western societies, this may contradict traditions and values in other societies in the world (Alston 1994). It has been argued, and rightly so, that the lack of specific standards connected to the principle of the 'best interests of the child' makes it possible to use this principle to legitimize a practice in one culture that in another would be seen as hurting children (Alston 1994). Following from this, notions of 'the best interests of the child' and participation rights are closely intertwined with cultural notions of a (good) childhood in a particular local context.

I will now turn the attention to a government policy document (Kindergartens in the Best Interests of Children and Parents) produced by the Ministry for Children and

Family Affairs,[3] which describes the political aims of kindergartens in Norway this way, reflecting how participation rights are interpreted:

> Children have to be children on their own terms, based on their own interests and they must be protected against adult control.
>
> (Ministry of Children and Family Affairs 1999–2000: 73)

This quote reflects how adults are seen as a threat to children's possibilities to exercise their rights to participation. This view is connected to an emphasis on 'children's own culture', where children are seen as different from adults. They are placed in an age-segregated social order and seen as a group of human beings inhabiting their 'own culture', characterized by play, creativity and activities developed together with their peers. This notion of children is close to what has been described as the 'tribal child' (James *et al.* 1998) where children are seen as a kind of 'indigenous people'. In Denmark and Norway discourses of 'the tribal child' have been powerful, also emphasizing children as 'natural beings', close to nature and enjoying 'free play' in particular outdoors (Kjørholt 2001, 2003; Nilsen 2010). The discourse of 'the tribal child' is closely connected to neoliberal discourses on participation as self-determination and increased individual freedom of choice, prevalent in Denmark and Norway since the 1990s. Discourses on young children as citizens and empirical studies in early childhood education and care in Norway and Denmark indicate a tendency to interpret rights to participate and citizenship as self-determination and rights to individual freedom of choice (Kjørholt 2005; Clark *et al.* 2005; Gulløv 2010; Kjørholt and Seland 2010). Based on studies in Denmark, Jan Kampmann argues that this is characteristic of the second period of institutionalization of children below school age (Kampmann 2004). As part of 'new' practices that were introduced in the project aimed at promoting children as citizens in Danish daycare centres in the early 1990s, the staff abolished former practices such as common meals for everybody, group activities arranged by the staff, such as storytelling, and others. These were seen as governed by adults and therefore not in line with children's rights to individual autonomy and freedom of choice. Individual self-determination and the right to practise 'their own culture' together with other children without adult intervention were core elements in the new practices. Toddlers were even given 'the right to decide when to change a new nappy' as part of being constituted as right claimers and competent citizens from an early age (Kjørholt 2005).

In several local political documents related to kindergartens in Norway since 2000, the concept 'the new kindergarten building' appears (see Trondheim Municipality 2005). This document reveals how discourses on children's rights to participation are linked to a shift also in the design and architecture of the kindergarten building:

> The current conceptualization of children is characterized by seeing children as competent, active, creative and explorative, being in need of a stimulating environment with many options to choose from regarding experience activity and learning. The environment needs to be characterized by the fact that children are going to

> participate in and actively influence everyday life. The design and furniture have to be planned in a way that promotes competence and own individual choice (taken by children).
>
> (Trondheim Municipality 2005: 16)

Flexible and larger groups of children are among the changes in the 'new kindergarten'. One new practice implemented is a kind of democratic forum; a 'children's meeting' every morning, which is aimed at promoting children's rights to active participation in everyday life and permit them an influence in decision-making processes in the kindergarten. In this meeting, 40 children aged two-and-a-half to six years old sit together and are asked one by one in which room they want to be in during the following two hours. It is emphasized that it is important for children to make their own decisions regarding choice of activity and playmates during the day (Kjørholt and Tingstad 2007). Democratic fora such as the 'children's meeting' represent a potential space for children to have influence in decision-making processes. However, there are certain paradoxes related to the new practice. While children in the previous kindergartens, with fixed units, were allowed to move freely and decide what to do, whom to play with and in which room to stay without formulating this in a 'children's meeting', the new practices in the flexible and new kindergarten building implies transforming the physical and social space for play and social relations with peers. In many ways the new space restricts children's possibilities for flexible movements and connectedness to others based on emotional experiences and spontaneous decisions in the here and now. By connecting participation rights to the practice of the 'children's meeting' first and foremost, the space of the kindergarten is connected to notions of children as rational human subjects, capable of formulating individual needs by verbal language. This is problematic, hiding the variety of different sensual, emotional and embodied languages of human beings. The opportunity to formulate individual wishes and views through verbal language represents *one*, but not *the only* way of human expression. Rights discourses are based on the Anglo-American liberal tradition, which constructs human beings as legal subjects capable of speaking for themselves and acting in their own interests. The subject is constructed as a rational autonomous individual, with the consciousness to formulate his or her own needs and wishes. Within these discourses, it has been argued that children are 'deemed to possess the autonomy and self-consciousness sufficient to be able to make rights claims' (Diduck 1999: 128).

Furthermore, studies of children's rights to participation expose that discourses on children are characterized by dichotomous notions of children, as either competent social actors with rights to autonomy on the one hand, or as vulnerable, independent and in need of care on the other (Kjørholt *et al.* 2005). Following from this, protection rights for children are seen as contradictory to participation rights and connected with the paradigm of children as dependent, vulnerable and incomplete compared to adults.

However, since participation rights were included in the new Kindergarten Act of 2006 and the revised national curriculum for early childhood education and care services in Norway, the Framework Plan of 2006, research voices arguing for a broader approach in regard to the implementation of participation rights in early childhood have been part of the debate (Bae 2009; Eide and Winger 2006; Johannesen and Sandvik 2008; Winger 2008). The discursive field is currently characterized by an increased openness to a variety of different forms of participation. An example that illustrates this is the project: Children's Participation in a Relational Perspective, a network-project including collaboration between kindergartens, universities and university colleges in Norway. The project, funded by the Research Council of Norway and led by Berit Bae, focuses on the youngest children in the kindergarten. Some of their objectives are to generate research-based knowledge about children as participants in everyday routines, play and learning activities in kindergartens, and to contribute to opportunities for kindergarten staff to critically reflect on their frames of reference and ways of being (Bae 2009). It is argued that in order to realize children's rights to influence and participation in early childhood services on children's own terms, the following points are important: support and follow up children's initiatives, be close to and respond to children with expressivity, support children's playfulness, and be capable of changing perspective and see the world from the children's point of view (Bae 2009). From a phenomenological perspective, studies demonstrate that toddlers create peer cultures in early childhood education and care institutions by engaging in joint bodily movements and emotional meaning-making processes, involving laughter, a particular rhythm and joy (Løkken 2000). In a recent publication, Nina Winger connects the discussion of children's participation rights to the quality of the institutional care. Quality, she argues, is reconstructed and constructed by all the social actors in the early childhood education and care setting every day. The social actors are all connected through relationships and belonging communities. The ability to express oneself, explore the environment and engage in play activities is closely interconnected with the establishing of a feeling of connectedness and belonging (Winger 2008).

Young children as citizens and the interrelatedness of rights

However, turning attention to the UNCRC again, the quotation from the UN Committee on the Rights of the Child in the introduction indicates that there are two opposing and dichotomous notions of young children, as either vulnerable and in need of socialization, or as competent human beings. The Committee speaks about a 'shift away from traditional beliefs that regard early childhood mainly as a period for the socialization of the immature human being'. However, when the Committee on the Rights of the Child further persuades states to create a positive agenda for implementing rights in early childhood, they recommend the parties to:

> ... encourage recognition of young children as social actors from the beginning of life, with particular interests, capacities and vulnerabilities, and of requirements for protection, guidance and support in the exercise of their rights.
>
> (UN Committee on the Rights of the Child 2006: 2)

At the same time as they are referring to a shift with regard to notions of young children, the quotation above reflects an emphasis on children's agency not in opposition to, but in compliance with, children's vulnerability. This is interesting and indicates a perspective where the different rights are seen as interrelated. In the General Comment from the UN Committee on the Rights of the Child, which was published in 2006, a holistic approach to rights is underlined, also pointing to the importance of play to ensure health and development:

> The Committee reminds States parties (and others concerned) that the right to survival and development can only be implemented in a holistic manner, through the enforcement of all the other provisions of the Convention, including rights to health, adequate nutrition, social security, an adequate standard of living, a healthy and safe environment, education and play (arts. 24, 27, 28, 29 and 31) ...
>
> (UN Committee on the Rights of the Child 2006: 4)

An interrelated approach to rights in early childhood also implies openness for a variety of different perspectives and practices related to the implementation of participation rights, and to what it means to be a competent social actor within early childhood education services. Young children's rights to play are among other things connected to adults' responsibilities to support children, to nurture them and provide them with emotional care and sensitive guidance.

Moreover, the parties' responsibilities to identify factors that prevent children from excitement, joy and play are highlighted. Poverty is mentioned as one important factor in this regard. That the Committee in their comments also connects the implementation of participation rights in article 12 to rights to play in article 31, is of particular interest:

> Planning for towns, and leisure and play facilities should take account of children's right to express their views (art. 12), through appropriate consultations. In all these respects, States parties are encouraged to pay greater attention and allocate adequate resources (human and financial) to the implementation of the right to rest, leisure and play.
>
> (UN Committee on the Rights of the Child 2006: 15)

The implementation of the UNCRC requires reflection on questions related to childhood and children's everyday lives in different contexts, including ideological, cultural and ethical evaluation of what it means to be a child and how a 'good' childhood is constituted. This point is also taken into account by the UN Committee, stating that variations regarding cultural expectations and treatment of children should be respected.

Autonomy and connectedness within diverse social contexts

As stated in Chapter 1, by Kernan, Singer and Swinnen, young children's relationships refers to 'children's interpersonal relationships with peers, younger and older children and adults in their everyday lives, at home and in the whole host of early childhood care and education settings'. They argue that the experience of positive social relations and the development of positive identities are core dimensions of children's well-being and sense of belonging (Brooker and Woodhead 2008; Dunn 2004; Singer and de Haan 2007). In addition, I will argue that agency and competence are in dynamic ways derived through participation in social practices within a web of social relationships. I have earlier argued that 'Inclusion, regardless of age or group membership, is dependent on a sense of self-being derived through active participation with, and belonging to other human beings' (Kjørholt 2008: 29). I will continue this rethinking of young children's rights to connectedness by drawing attention to different ways of listening to young children.

The variety of landscapes of childhoods is created through relationships. Listening to young children implies being involved in social meaning-making together, to engage in cognitive and emotional processes contributing to the construction of the landscape of childhood in individual children as well as in groups of children. The landscapes of childhood consist of pictures, images, colours, smells and sounds, being embedded in and carrying the human being through the life course. These images, which I think all of us are able to reactivate at least to a certain extent, are memories that are supposed to represent pillars of self-confidence and trust, sources of vitality and passion, and a reservoir of meaning. They also evoke a whole register of different emotions, covering anxiety, sadness, tears, fears and dark memories. Embedded in the human mind and body, as cultural lags of consciousness, these images represent an emotional repertoire for acting and communicating. A challenge for all human beings through the life course is to listen to and be connected to our own inner voices, as sources to connect to other people in caring communities. By this, a democratic ethos is created in minds and bodies from an early age. In rights discourses there is a danger of excluding the embodied subject and thus the embodied expressions that are vital in order to understand and recognize children as human beings. It is pertinent to pay attention to the 'unspoken words', the huge complexity of bodily movements and emotional expressions, by which children construct their identities and social practices in everyday life.

Working with children in early childhood, it is also important to develop a differentiated approach, covering a wide range of diverse 'styles' from storytelling as sources of inspiration for dialogue and reflection, the expressive activities such as drawing, painting, musical performances and others, to participant observation with groups of children as a way to learn to understand everyday life the way children experience and perceive it. Philosophy for young children, stimulating and nourishing children's thoughts, questions and reflections about life and being in the world, represents an additional and exciting approach in relation to early childhood education and care services, embracing children's rights to autonomy and connectedness as closely intertwined processes. This approach is also connected to the argument made by Peter Moss in a recent publication, asserting that dependency is untheorized, and that there is a need for reconceptualization of the relationship between dependency, autonomy, respect and democracy (Moss 2009).

Concluding remarks

Dependency does not only refer to social relations, but also to dependency of a particular cultural context. Constructing early childhood education and care services as democratic and social spaces for autonomy, belonging and connectedness, also means connecting to the local social and cultural context in which the institution is placed. There is a lack of knowledge related to childhood and children's everyday lives in non-Western contexts, as these are conceptualized and practised. Based on research in South Asia it has been argued that respect for young children and their views do not lead to lack of respect for parents (George 2009). Local knowledge and social practices regarding notions of childcare, generational relations, family life, emotions and embodied language, including music and other forms of art, the meaning of rituals, religious beliefs and practices, etc., can be seen as a source of knowledge to be reflected in the daily life in the institution. If we can get beyond – though not reject – the rights-based discourse of listening, we can open up to listening as a concept of many possibilities, which applies not just to young children, but to older children and adults of all ages (Moss *et al.* 2005). These approaches open for a vision of early childhood education and care services not only as a resource centre and social space for young children, but as social and inclusive spaces for belonging and connectedness embracing different age groups.

Point for reflection and discussion

Every state that has ratified the United Nations Convention on the Rights of the Child is required to report to the Committee on the Rights of the Child on how it is fulfilling its human rights obligations. How are young children represented in your country's report to the Committee? Compare the issues raised with those discussed by Kjørholt in this chapter.

Notes

1 Anne Trine Kjørholt is director of the Norwegian Centre for Child Research. She and her colleagues conduct research that is theoretically and methodologically related to the paradigm of the interdisciplinary social studies of children and childhood. The centre is a key institution for the global research network Childwatch International. Among the recent larger research projects that the author is managing are: (1) The Modern Child and the Flexible Labour Market. Institutionalization and Individualization of Children's Lives; (2) Children as Citizens and the Best Interest of the Child; (3) Children, Young People and Local Knowledge in Ethiopia and Zambia.

2 Kindergarten is a daycare centre for children below school age, one to six years old. In recent years there has been an extensive expansion of kindergarten places due to a high priority on the political agenda. Today 90 per cent of all children in early childhood are offered a kindergarten place.

3 This Ministry of Children and Equality had until 2007 the national responsibility for the kindergartens in Norway. In 2007 there was a shift, and the kindergartens are now under the administration of the Ministry of Education and Research.

Bibliography

Alston, P. (1994) 'The best interests principle: towards a reconciliation of culture and human rights'. In P. Alston (ed.) *The Best Interests of the Child: Reconciling Culture and Human Rights*. Oxford: Clarendon Press.

Bae, B. (2009) 'Children's right to participate – challenges in everyday interactions'. *European Early Childhood Education Research Journal*, 17(3): 391–406.

Bartley, K. (1998) 'Barnpolitik och barns rettigheter' *(Child politics and children's rights)*. Unpublished PhD thesis. Gøteborg: Sosiologiska Institutionen.

Brembeck, H., Johansson, B. and Kampmann, J. (eds) (2004) *Beyond the Competent Child: Exploring Contemporary Childhoods in the Nordic Welfare Societies*. Roskilde: Roskilde University Press.

Brooker, L. and Woodhead, M. (2008) *Developing Positive Identities: Diversity and Young Children*. Milton Keynes: The Open University.

Clark, A., Kjørholt, A.T. and Moss, P. (eds) (2005) *Beyond Listening. Children's Perspectives in Early Childhood Services*. Bristol: The Policy Press.

Corsaro, W. (2003) *We're Friends, Right? Inside Kid's Culture*. Washington D.C.: Joseph Henry Press.

Dahlberg, G. and Moss, P. (2005) *Ethics and Politics in Early Childhood Education*. London: Routledge Falmer.

Diduck, A. (1999) 'Justice and childhood: reflections on refashioned boundaries'. In M. King (ed) *Moral Agendas for Children's Welfare*. London: Routledge.

Dunn, J. (2004) *Children's Friendships: The Beginnings of Intimacy*. Oxford: Blackwell.

Eide, B. and Winger, N. (2006) 'Dilemmaer ved barns medvirkning' [Dilemmas with children's participation]. In B. Bae, B. Eide, A.-E. Kristoffersen and N. Winger, *Temahefte om barns medvirkning [Special Issue on Children's Participation]*. Oslo: Ministry of Education.

George, S. (2009) Too young for respect? Realising respect for young children in their everyday environments. A cross–cultural analysis. Working Papers in Early Childhood Development, No. 54. The Hague, The Netherlands: Bernard van Leer Foundation.

Gulløv, E. (2003) 'Creating a natural place for children: an ethnographic study of Danish kindergartens'. In K.F. Olwig and E. Gulløv (eds) *Children's Places: Cross-Cultural Perspectives*. London: Routledge.

——(forthcoming, 2010) 'Kindergartens in Denmark – reflections on continuity and change'. In A.T. Kjørholt and J. Qvortrup (eds) *The Modern Child and the Flexible Labour Market: Exploring Early Childhood Education and Care*. Hampshire: Palgrave Macmillan.

James, A., Jenks, C. and Prout, A. (1998) *Theorizing Childhood*. Cambridge: Polity Press.

Johannesen, N. and Sandvik, N. (2008) *Små barns medvirkning – noen perspektiver [Young Children's Participation – Some Perspectives]*. Oslo: Cappelen-Damm.

Kampmann, J. (2004) 'Societalization of childhood: new opportunities? new demands?'. In H. Brembeck, B. Johansson and J. Kampmann (eds) *Beyond the Competent Child: Exploring Contemporary Childhoods in the Nordic Welfare Societies*. Roskilde: Roskilde University Press.

Kjørholt, A.T. (2001) 'The participating child – a vital pillar in this century?'. *Nordic Educational Research*, 21(2): 65–81.

——(2003) 'Imagined communities': the local community as a place for 'children's culture' and social participation in Norway'. In Olwig, K.F. and Gulløv, E. (eds) *Children's Places. Cross-cultural Perspectives*. London: Routledge, pp. 197–216.

——(2005) 'The competent child and the "right to be oneself": reflections on children as fellow citizens in an early childhood centre'. In A. Clark, A.T. Kjørholt and P. Moss (eds) *Beyond Listening. Children's Perspectives on Early Childhood Services*. Bristol: The Policy Press.

——(2008) 'Children as new citizens: in the best interests of the child'. In A. James and A. James (eds) *European Childhoods: Cultures, Politics and Childhoods in the European Union*. Hampshire: Palgrave Macmillan.

Kjørholt, A.T., Moss, P. and Clark, A. (2005) 'Beyond listening: future prospects'. In A. Clark, A.T. Kjørholt and P. Moss (eds) *Beyond Listening. Children's Perspectives on Early Childhood Services.* Bristol: The Policy Press.

Kjørholt, A.T. and Tingstad, V. (2007) 'Flexible places for flexible children? Discourses on the new kindergarten architecture'. In H. Zeiher, D. Devine, A.T. Kjørholt and H. Strandell (eds) *Flexible Childhood? Exploring Children's Welfare in Time and Space. Cost Action A19: Children's Welfare, Vol. 2.* Odense: University Press of Southern Denmark.

Kjørholt, A.T. and Seland, M. (forthcoming, 2010) 'Kindergarten as a bazaar: freedom of choice and new forms of regulation'. In A.T. Kjørholt and J. Qvortrup (eds) *The Modern Child and the Flexible Labour Market: Exploring Early Childhood Education and Care.* Hampshire: Palgrave Macmillan.

Løkken, G. (2000) 'Toddler peer culture: the social style of one and two year old body-subjects in everyday interaction'. Unpublished PhD thesis. Trondheim: Norwegian University of Science and Technology.

Ministry of Children and Family Affairs (1999–2000) *White Paper No. 27. Daycare centres do the best for children and parents.* Oslo: Barne-og familiedepartementet.

——(2006) *Kindergarten Act of 2005-06-17-64.* Oslo: Barne-og familiedepartementet.

Ministry of Education and Research (2006) *Framework Plan for the Content and Tasks of Kindergartens.* Oslo: Kunnskaps-og forskningsdepartementet.

Mortier, F. (2002) 'The meaning of individualisation for children's citizenship'. In F. Mouritsen and J. Qvortrup (eds) *Childhood and Children's Culture.* Odense: University Press of Southern Denmark.

Moss, P. (2009) 'There are alternatives! Markets and democratic experimentalism in early childhood education and care'. Working Paper in Early Childhood Development, No. 53. The Hague, the Netherlands: Bernard van Leer Foundation.

Moss, P., Clark, A. and Kjørholt, A.T. (2005) 'Introduction'. In A. Clark, A.T. Kjørholt and P. Moss (eds) *Beyond Listening. Children's Perspectives on Early Childhood Services.* Bristol: The Policy Press.

Näsman, E. (1994) 'Individualization and institutionalization of childhood in today's Europe'. In J. Qvortrup, M. Bardy, G. Sgritta and H. Wintersberger (eds) *Childhood Matters Social Theory, Practice and Politics.* Aldershot: Avebury.

Nilsen, R.D. (forthcoming, 2010) 'Flexible spaces – flexible subjects in nature. Transcending the "fenced" childhood in day-care centres?'. In A.T. Kjørholt and J. Qvortrup (eds) *The Modern Child and the Flexible Labour Market: Exploring Early Childhood Education and Care.* Hampshire: Palgrave Macmillan.

Rinaldi, C. (2005) 'Documentation and assessment: what is the relationship?'. In A. Clark, A.T. Kjørholt and P. Moss (eds) *Beyond Listening. Children's Perspectives on Early Childhood Services.* Bristol: The Policy Press.

Seland, M. (2009) 'The modern child and the flexible daycare center. An ethnographic study of consequences of new discourses and new public management for everyday life in Norwegian daycare'. Unpublished PhD thesis. Trondheim: Norwegian University of Science and Technology, Norwegian Centre for Child Research.

Singer, E. and de Haan, D. (2007) *The Social Lives of Young Children: Play Conflict and Moral Learning in Day-Care Groups.* Amsterdam: B.V. Uitgeverij SWP.

Trondheim Municipality (2005) *Funksjons-og arealprogram for kommunale barnehager i Trondheim* [*Function and area program for municipal kindergartens in Trondheim*]. Trondheim: Trondheim Municipality.

UN Committee on the Rights of the Child (2006) *General Comment No. 7. Implementing child rights in early childhood.* (CRC/C/GC/7/Rev.1, 20 September 2006).

Winger, N. (2008) 'Kvalitet, medvirkning og etikk' [Quality, participation and ethics]. *Barnehagefolk* 2: 17–25.

Chapter 5

Play and prescription

The impact of national developments in England

Tricia David, Kathy Goouch and Sacha Powell[1]

Introduction

In this chapter we present an analysis of the current situation concerning young children and their opportunities to play with peers in England. The new curriculum for children from birth to five – the *Early Years Foundation Stage* (EYFS) (Department for Education and Skills 2007) contains a 54-page document of legal requirements for early childhood education and care (ECEC) providers, together with other practice guidance. Although this policy document purports to emphasize the role of play, further document analysis reveals continuing contradictory Government messages, which create tensions between policy and practice. England, like several other countries (for example, the United States and the Netherlands) remains gripped by the belief that ECEC should prepare children for primary school through early admission to settings with greater emphasis on formal, teacher-planned and directed learning. Opportunities to play with other children, to be agents in their own learning, forging and enjoying peer relationships – friendships – and to become confident and at ease in interactions with others, are thus endangered in ECEC settings, schools and the wider community. We explain that some early years teachers attempt to overcome these policy contradictions through *creative compliance,* while other highly skilled and committed colleagues adopt a *relational pedagogy*, which enables young children to play and learn as participants in a community of learners.

Children in England: the state of play in the wider community

Perhaps as a response to reports (e.g. Hillman *et al.* 2000; Layard and Dunn 2009) highlighting the comparative unhappiness and increasingly limited freedom of England's children, the Government in England published its first national *Play Strategy*, earmarking £235 million to:

> make sure that every residential area has a variety of high-quality places for all children to play safely and free of charge … [as] a direct response to demands from children, young people and their families for better play facilities.
>
> (Department for Children, Schools and Families 2008a: 3)

At last, legitimization through national policy helps to raise the profile of play's importance in children's lives, and cash-strapped providers and maintainers of play spaces have welcomed the dedicated funding. Play is defined by the Department for Children, Schools and Families (2008a: 11) as:

> children and young people following their own ideas and interests, in their own way and for their own reasons, having fun while respecting themselves and others.

But deeper analysis of the policy discourse reveals a worrying emphasis on containment and control of where, how and to some extent when children have opportunities to play and, therefore, with what and with whom (Powell 2008). Indeed, the Director of Play England, the independent body that spearheaded the campaign for a national strategy and now leads its implementation, has stated that:

> If the vision is realised, this should lead, in time, to community space ... where children can play without being seen as a nuisance ... it will require a huge buy-in from planners, and remains to be seen if this will be forthcoming ... there are of course prejudices against young people to overcome.
>
> (*The Guardian* 2008)

Until this vision becomes a reality, children's play opportunities are still largely restricted to designated spaces. An objective of the Play Strategy is 'to improve opportunities for all children [in] places where children and young people spend their leisure time (including parks and green spaces), schools and Sure Start Children's Centres' (Department for Children, Schools and Families 2008a: 7).

However, despite the 2004 Children Act's statutory duty for local (and national) government bodies to take account of the views of children when they plan services, there is little evidence that the youngest children are included. For example, more than 9,000 children were involved in the Fair Play consultation on the Play Strategy (Department for Children, Schools and Families 2008b) but the majority responded using online tools. Although figures concerning the ages of children are not given, it seems improbable that very young children were involved in this type of consultation. In a much bigger local government exercise (42,800 respondents aged 19 and under) in England's most populous, non-metropolitan county children over seven were invited to give their views about the areas in which they live, rest and play and the services provided for them (Office of National Statistics 2001 census figures). While this is to be applauded, the views of the local population of more than 130,000 children aged from birth to seven years, constituting 39 per cent of those 19 years and under were not surveyed.

The youngest children are, therefore, most likely to access (public) play opportunities in ECEC settings and thus, according to the Play Strategy, these settings need to provide an environment and ethos that upholds their right to play, offers them choice and respects their agency in making those choices. The Government's headline policy language claims it is doing all these things, but a closer inspection of documents and practices reveals a different picture.

Play and curricula for young children in England

Each of the countries that make up the United Kingdom (UK) – England, Scotland, Wales and Northern Ireland – has now gone its own way in relation to the governance of provision for young children. In England, fears are heightened concerning potential negative effects on young children's enjoyment of childhood and learning resulting from the legal requirement for providers of ECEC to comply with the demands of the Government's EYFS (Department for Education and Skills 2007) and the National Curriculum in primary schools (which includes children from five to seven) (Department for Education and Employment/Qualifications and Curriculum Authority 1999). Both contain detailed, prescribed curricula and outcomes, which create a restrictive context (British Educational Research Association Early Years Special Interest Group 2003; Evans 2009) and 'potentially overpower the intentions of the child' (Goouch 2009: 142). The difficulties related to these limitations have been particularly marked in Year R (reception) classes of primary school (British Educational Research Association Early Years Special Interest Group 2003; Broadhead 2004).

Thus, critics claim that play is being sidelined in favour of an emphasis on adult direction and that the curriculum is inappropriately pre-primary rather than socio-cultural (Bennett 2005; Evans 2009). Does this mean that children's opportunities for play with peers are diminished as a result of the imposition of detailed national regulation?

The development of the EYFS

Children in England have been required by law to attend school from the age of five years[2] and during the last century much of that schooling involved sitting and being taught formally, despite the influence of respected pioneers of early education, such as Froebel, Owen, Montessori, Steiner, the MacMillan sisters and Isaacs, who advocated the adoption of approaches involving children in play and exploration until at least the age of seven. Their ideas did, however, permeate nursery education where it existed. Nationally funded education for children under five was limited in England until late in the 20th century, because young children were regarded as the responsibility of their parents. Even now parents must pay the total cost of ECEC for children from birth to two years. A small number of two year olds defined as needing support are granted some part-time ECEC free of charge, as are most children aged three and four. During the academic year in which they become five the majority of young children attend primary school reception classes in maintained (state-funded) schools, full time and free of charge.

The majority of nursery provision in England continues to be run by either private or voluntary groups or individuals. In the past, successive Governments were reluctant to institute any form of national curriculum for children under five, since a curriculum might imply an entitlement and the expectation of Government funding. Unfortunately the effect of this situation has been that young children and their families continue to experience wide variations in access to and quality of ECEC provision, including the misconception among many workers in the sector traditionally labelled 'care' that 'education' means formal instruction.

During the last ten years there has been greater recognition worldwide for lifelong learning (OECD 2001, 2006). In England, a succession of Government legislation, funding, research and a project culminating in a pack to support those working with children from birth to three years (Department for Education and Skills 2003; David *et al.* 2003) have most recently come to fruition in the EYFS (Department for Education and Skills 2007), under the auspices of *Every Child Matters* (Department for Education and Skills 2004).

The EYFS includes a *Statutory Framework* (a statement of legal requirements), as well as *Practice Guidance and Principles*, for ECEC providers, teachers of children in the reception year of primary school, parents and others, such as trainers, involved with children in the birth to five age group. Within the *Statutory Framework*, 13 assessment scales are set out. These cover:

Personal, Social and Emotional Development
Communication, Language and Literacy
Problem Solving, Reasoning and Numeracy
Knowledge and Understanding of the World
Physical Development
Creative Development

Practitioners are expected to maintain written records of each child's progress and achievements, and they may use the official *Early Years Foundation Stage Profile* booklet.

The *Statutory Framework* also states that:

> Providers must plan and organise their systems to ensure that every child receives an enjoyable and challenging learning and development experience that is tailored to meet their individual needs … that there is a balance of adult-led and freely chosen or child-initiated activities, delivered through indoor and outdoor play.
> (Department for Education and Skills 2007: 37).

Thus, by law, play and choice are fundamental aspects of early years provision for children under five – but how will 'balance' and 'adult-led activities' be interpreted? Indeed, are practitioners universally competent in planning for, observing and, where appropriate, intervening or joining in child-led play?

An analysis of the legal requirements of the EYFS curriculum in relation to play and learning

The EYFS *Statutory Framework* contains 20 management-style references to play, none requiring practice that fosters joint play with other children. The *Practice Guidance,* the *Principles into Practice* cards and other supplementary material do contain suggestions relating to playing with other children, but regulatory systems have often failed to acknowledge the centrality of relationships in ECEC (David 1999). Further anxieties revolve around pressure resulting from the inclusion of learning goals, especially those concerned with phonic knowledge, reading and writing, or from practitioners' perceptions of the expectations of the Office for Standards in Education – OFSTED – inspectors (David *et al.* 2000; Bennett 2005).

The EYFS *Statutory Framework* (Department for Education and Skills 2007), as outlined earlier, 'sets the standards for learning, development and care for children from 0–5 years' and its aims include 'laying a secure foundation for future learning through learning and development that is planned around the individual needs and *interests* of the child' (p.7 our italics). Deeper analysis of this document reveals much more contradictory messages both about play and about children's choice and agency in their play and learning.

Practitioners are advised, for example, that their assessments of children's progress towards meeting the 'early learning goals' should be made through observation of children's behaviour and 'predominantly children's self-initiated activities' (p.16). Indeed, research has shown that it is during freely chosen play that children manifest the highest levels of their abilities and the implication is that assessment can best capture children's learning and development during these activities. However, a search through the *Framework* for examples of 'planned, purposeful play' (p.11), a contradiction in itself, reveals that among the 54 pages and 19,700 words:

there is only one reference to children's *choice*
'Reads books of own choice' (p.45);

there is only one reference to *opportunity*
'They must be provided with opportunity and encouragement to use their skills' (p.12);

there are three references to children's *preference(s)*, for example:
'Providers must obtain information … [about] special dietary requirements, preferences or food allergies' (p.22);

and three child-related references to children *selecting*, including two versions of:
'Build and construct with a wide range of objects, *selecting* appropriate resources' (p.14 and p.46, our italics).

Similar words indicating agency or choice (want, decide, desire, wish, opt) are equally sparse or non-existent with reference to children. In contrast, there are 116 uses of learn/learning, 59 references to assess/assessment, and 28 references to goals.

Children's rights: play with peers and the impact of the EYFS

Several Articles of the United Nations Convention on the Rights of the Child (United Nations 1989) could be seen as relevant in relation to this issue, particularly Article 12, which requires states to 'assure to the child who is capable of forming his or her own views the right to express those views freely'. However, unless children are given opportunities to exercise choice and to express their ideas, they will be unable to enact this right. Making choices, negotiating with peers, and actively participating and reflecting on consequences contribute to children's cognitive, social and emotional development, as well as 'using play as a (communicative) *resource for participating in everyday life*' (author's italics; Strandell 2000: 149).

The analysis described earlier indicates that the *Framework* suggests children's right to play in ECEC settings is a right that is confined to a utilitarian role in achieving early learning goals, and the *Guidance* offers little encouragement for practitioners to respect children's *agency* in enacting their right to play and making choices about and in their play. To overcome this policy discourse, some practitioners encourage children's agency by developing a pedagogy of 'creative compliance' (Lambirth and Goouch 2006), presenting children with playful activities they may enjoy but over which they have no control.

Play and learning

Theorists and researchers have explored young children's play and its importance as an approach to early childhood education for many years. In England some of the most influential during the last century have been Piaget, Vygotsky, Bruner, Hutt, Tizard and Sutton-Smith. Work by neuroscientists such as Blakemore (2000), Gopnik *et al.* (1999) and Trevarthen (1998), has contributed to thinking about play and learning.

Defining play is problematic (Nutbrown 2006), and some researchers argue it is easier to say what play is not. Bruce (2005) prefers to use the term 'free-flow play', suggesting its characteristics include being active; controlled by the player; intrinsically motivated; lacking external pressure; sensitive paired, grouped or solitary activity; an integrating mechanism in a child's learning. Similarly, Broadhead (2004) argues that young children need time, space and, sometimes, specific meaningful objects, but above all agency, to build momentum in joint play narratives.

Emphasis on play is not without its critics, however. For example, the Western/northern assumption that playing in a nursery is preferable to working is justified for extreme, hazardous, exploitative situations, but in some societies the interactions afforded by employment may be viewed as contributing to a child's socialization (Woodhead 2005).

Perhaps another problem with today's English lifestyles is the paucity of opportunities for children to spend time playing in mixed age groups. Other issues involve exclusion, where some children control play bouts in ways that prevent others from taking part, or even involve threatening, negative behaviours (Wood 2007). Clearly these demand practitioners' intervention enabling excluded children to participate meaningfully and working with families, explaining the approach and listening to parents' views, with adults and children exploring together how to ensure no one's rights are being infringed (Wall 2006).

Meanwhile, learning, put simply, is the acquisition of knowledge or skill. In psychological terms, it means a change has occurred in the brain and/or behaviour. So learning and play are not synonymous. Further, Hutt *et al.* (1989) suggested that during these early years, play behaviours exhibit two forms – *epistemic* (a serious search for knowledge about something – or someone – 'What does this or s/he do?') and *ludic* (playfully exploring what one can do with that knowledge – 'What can I do with this?').

The extent to which formal instruction is considered necessary will relate to adult understandings about the complexity of the curriculum, the processes through which young children learn and are able to comprehend, and educators' knowledge of the children's earlier experience and achievements.

Major government-funded research projects of the last two decades (Sylva *et al.* 2004; Siraj-Blatchford *et al.* 2002) have advised early childhood educators that there should be a balance of adult-led and child-led activities, as reiterated in the *Statutory Framework* (Department for Education and Skills 2007). Anxious practitioners have asked about this balance and its inherent dualism. The approach known as *relational*, or *dialogic, pedagogy* (Papatheodorou and Moyles 2009), which is informed by cues from the children, is a way out of this dualistic dilemma because it entails communities of learners engaging actively in relationships by pursuing knowledge together.

The role of adults in children's play

Dualistic dilemmas abound. Working with young children is complex and multi-layered. Yet, quite rightly, government agencies expect that those working with children in any context and at any stage should be accountable for their practice. Among this duality – the complex nature of early years education and political accountability – there are adults who are daily in the company of young children, forging relationships and working to understand the development and learning needs of each child in their care. However, as soon as politics and education become entwined then outcomes, targets, simple measures and media sound bites tend to take centre stage (Sachs 2003) and, in England, we struggle with the crucial issue of 'who controls the field of judgement' (Ball 2004: 143) and how we understand professionalism and professional judgement. Also, in England, we are sensitive to the terms used to describe adults working with young children. They are variously teachers, practitioners, nursery assistants, nursery nurses and teaching assistants. How society labels and defines those who work with children must invariably help to determine the professional identity they then assume. While 'teacher' is often mistakenly used synonymously with 'instructor' this label/identity simply will not suffice in early years education.

Pressures on professionals working in ECEC in relation to performativity (Ball 2004) often result in activities being created for children by early years educators, leading to pre-ordained curricular outcomes, frequently exhausting the majority of young children's time in nurseries and schools. While young children come into ECEC settings with their own play intentions, some teachers/practitioners arrive with designs on the shape and outcome of children's play in order to fulfil political aims and Government intentions. Thus any activities that occur within the walls of schools or nurseries are often adult designed, managed, reshaped or sometimes completely hijacked in order that teachers may use the occasion to account for targets and outcomes that in turn reflect on their professionalism. This has now become clearly expected of teachers:

> We now operate within a baffling array of figures, performance indicators, comparisons and competitions – in such a way that the contentments of stability are increasingly elusive, purposes are contradictory, motivations blurred and self worth slippery.
>
> (Ball 2004: 144)

That is, teachers are judged by their ability to perform in particular ways, achieving particular outcomes with the children in their care. The potential harmony Nias (1989: 44) described 20 years ago between self-image, place of work and what the work itself involved – 'a sense of fit' between values and the work context – appears almost irrelevant. In contemporary educational contexts Ball describes how we 'fabricate ourselves ... produce versions of ourselves ... choreograph performance' in order to achieve publicly acceptable results' (Ball 2004: 149).

It is hard to understand how such inauthenticity could be possible in work with young children. Most young children, however, are compliant and eager to collaborate with adults, seeking partnerships and dialogic opportunities. Bernstein claimed that teachers were employing play for 'surveillance', which in turn provided the opportunity for 'the spontaneity of the child [to be] filtered through this surveillance and then implicitly shaped according to interpretation, evaluation and diagnosis' (Bernstein 1997: 60). Through absorbing the current statutory requirements, play is now viewed by those working with them as a professional opportunity for accountability rather than as a spontaneous act of childhood. As discussed earlier, the term 'play' itself has now become part of the political discourse used to legislate for early years education in England. How this is understood and translated by practitioners is often problematic with some engaging in 'structural and individual schizophrenia' (Ball 2004: 146) and others becoming highly successful 'restricted professionals' (Hall 2004: 48), identifying what central and local government agencies require.

Building communities of learners, players and friends

There are those in early years education and care settings, however, who appear to understand the dilemma and the dualistic nature of their role and are confident in developing a respectful, relational pedagogy while still maintaining the kinds of records of learning and development that are statutorily required. Such professionals, though, are now rare, as teachers lean towards both the performativity culture described above and the idea that they should attend to the discourse of 'official science' (Wertsch 1991: 137). Where they do exist, such expert relational teachers are able to identify their professional purposes and, importantly, can clearly determine their own role in their work with young children, while they are playing.

Central to this way of working with young children is the knowledge that children can be trusted to learn when it matters to them to do so. Thus the creation of an early learning environment that presents opportunities, possibilities for play; an affective environment where children and their intentions drive adults' roles; where relationships are forged as children's developing intersubjectivity is fostered; is all dependent on a deep knowledge about children and the ever-developing understanding of early years educators as they play with, watch and listen to the children in their care.

Malaguzzi (2004) claimed that 'rich' teachers are born only out of their relationships with 'rich' children. Here, teachers engaging in organic, relational pedagogies are at least already awake to children's potential, to their intentions, giving more status to what they may learn *from* children than to governmental instructions to instruct or the development of ways to creatively comply with an inauthentic approach to teaching and learning. The richness described by Malaguzzi may simply relate to the fact that, in their work and in their own lived lives in families, such relational pedagogues view children as people. Children can then be liked, respected, related to; can become co-players, co-constructors, can be listened to and attended to; can be helped and supported; and their views and voices can be heard. Such an affective pedagogy is a bold step away from current political rhetoric in relation to education where the 'commodification' of expressive and affective curricular aims may take place only if it satisfies the needs of the 'knowledge economy' (Hartley 2006: 69).

Fifty years ago Piaget (1959: xix) discussed 'the art of teaching', describing the artistry with which teachers responded to children's talk while they created 'collective monologues'. This kind of skilful responsiveness requires teachers to be alert to the worlds in which children find themselves in their play and Piaget's research demonstrated how 'words thrown out are caught on the bounce, like balls' (Piaget 1959:13) by such skilled practitioners. In this way, children's intentions are served as teachers respond and contribute at the learner's point of need. The idea that teachers can be best employed by 'servicing' children's play may perhaps be contentious at a moment in history when 'teaching' is often used synonymously with 'instruction'. In a previous study (Goouch 2008), one teacher was insistent that 'their [children's] learning belongs to them and I have a role in helping to build learning and development but it isn't mine to build, it's theirs'. Such a shift in the power balance between adult and child can be witnessed when teachers feel confident to allow children's agency, when they see their role as servicing play and players and when they are sensitive in their responses, guided by their knowledge of children in general and specifically by the knowledge of the children in their care. Thus, in the words of the same teacher, 'the more our interactions fit in with the child, the more likely that they will be of use to the child, in developing and extending, understanding whatever it is they are exploring'.

In the recent political history of education in England it seems that teachers have been 'regarded as blank slates, or "palimpsests", tablets on which successive scripts are written' (Bryan 2004: 143) as each new initiative, guidance document or policy statement is crafted and inspection regimes set to ensure they are enacted. However, some teachers have escaped such Government conscription – is this because they are working with the youngest children or because of who they are, as people and as teachers? Teachers cannot be said to be of one 'kind'. It seems undeniable, however, that those teachers who both know children well and notice them at play are able to enrich learning experiences and support learning.

Children's minds, their development and their learning are not shaped by such good teachers but instead teaching, learning and development, and indeed teachers also, are themselves shaped by children as they play and, importantly, play with other children. Dunn (2004: 160) stresses friendship is 'the crucible in which so much learning about the social world – and indeed about ourselves – is likely to take place' and Martin's (2005: 231) study of happiness concludes that

> personal relationships are absolutely central to happiness and health ... a good education is one that fosters ... social and emotional competence, ... resilience and a lifelong love of learning ... Let children play.

We conclude, therefore, that nationally stated educational aims in England, that all children should have basic functional literacy and numeracy skills at the earliest opportunity to fulfil long-term political and economic goals, should *not* be pursued at the expense of children's happiness, well-being and long-term learning. Further, this is supported by a report of the most comprehensive review of primary education for 40 years, published today as we finalize our chapter (Alexander 2009). From our own and others' research, we know it to be possible to address educational aims through enabling young children to play, to express themselves, to make choices, develop agency and autonomy, and by helping them to make and sustain friendships – and teachers in England need support as they learn to play too.

Point for reflection and discussion

The authors analyze educational policy in England with regard to preparation for formal schooling and young children's opportunities to play. They point to the dual role of teachers. What do they mean by 'dual role'? Do you recognize this phenomenon in your own country or region? Interview two teachers in an early childhood education setting working with three-, four- or five-year-olds: do they experience dual role expectations? How do they deal with that?

Notes

1 Sacha Powell, Kathy Goouch and Tricia David are members of the early childhood research community in the south east of England, based at Canterbury Christ Church University. Each team member has been involved in a wide range of research projects nationally and internationally. Individually they represent different specialisms and interests in the field of early childhood education and care. In particular: Sacha – children's rights; Kathy – literacy; Tricia – policy and practice. Collectively they seek to make research findings and responses to national policy accessible to a broad range of audiences and to demonstrate the importance of research in underpinning all our work with young children.

2 Schooling is compulsory from the age of five but in practice most children attend school from the September of the academic year in which they will become five.

Bibliography

Alexander, R. (ed) (2009) *Children, their World, their Education: Final Report of the Cambridge Primary Review.* London: Routledge.

Ball, S.J. (ed) (2004) *The Routledge/Falmer Reader in Sociology of Education*. London: Routledge/Falmer.

Bennett, J. (2005) 'Curriculum issues in national policy-making'. *European Early Childhood Research Journal*, 13: 5–23.

Bernstein, B. (1997) 'Class and pedagogies: visible and invisible'. In A.H. Halsley, H. Lauder, P. Brown and A. S. Wells (eds) *Education, Culture, Economy, Society*. Oxford: Oxford University Press.

Blakemore, S.J. (2000) *Early Years Learning*. Report no.140 (June). London: Parliamentary Office of Science and Technology.

British Educational Research Association Early Years Special Interest Group (2003) *Early Years Research: Pedagogy, Curriculum and Adult Roles, Training and Professionalism*. Southwell Notts: BERA.

Broadhead, P. (2004) *Early Years Play and Learning*. London: Routledge Falmer.

Bruce, T. (2005) 'Play, the universe and everything'. In J. Moyles (ed) *The Excellence of Play*. Maidenhead: Open University Press.

Bryan, H. (2004) 'Constructs of teacher professionalism within a changing literacy landscape'. *Literacy*, 38: 141–8.

David, T. (ed) (1999) *Teaching Young Children*. London: PCP/Sage.

David, T., Raban, B., Ure, C., Goouch, K., Jago, M. and Barriere, J. (2000) *Making Sense of Early Literacy: A Practioner's Perspective*. Stoke-on-Trent: Trentham Books.

David, T., Goouch, K., Powell, S. and Abbott, L. (2003) *Birth to Three Matters: a review of the literature*. London: Department for Education and Skills. Research Report 444.

Department for Children, Schools and Families (2008a) *The Play Strategy*. Nottingham: Department for Children, Schools and Families Publications.

——(2008b) *Fair Play: A Consultation on the Play Strategy*. Nottingham: DCSF Publications.

Department for Education and Employment/Qualifications and Curriculum Authority (1999) *The National Curriculum*. London: DfEE/QCA.

Department for Education and Skills (2003) *Birth to Three Matters*. London: DfES/Sure Start Unit.

——(2004) *Every Child Matters: Change for Children*. London: DfES/HM Government.

——(2007) *Early Years Foundation Stage*. Nottingham: DfES Publications.

Dunn, J. (2004) *Children's Friendships*. Oxford: Blackwell.

Evans, M. (2009) 'Government signals end to target culture'. *Nursery World*, 9 July 2009: 10–11.

Goouch, K. (2008) 'Narratives of experience in the lives of teachers of young children'. Unpublished PhD thesis. University of Kent, Canterbury.

——(2009) 'Forging and fostering relationships in play: whose zone is it anyway?' In T. Papatheodorou and J. Moyles (eds) *Learning Together in the Early Years*. pp.139–52.

Gopnik, A., Melzoff, A. and Kuhl, P. (1999) *How Babies Think*. London: Weidenfeld and Nicolson.

Hall, K. (2004) *Literacy and Schooling, Towards Renewal in Primary Education Policy*. Hampshire: Ashgate.

Hartley, D. (2006) 'The instrumentalization of the expressive in education'. In A. Moore (ed) *Schooling, Society and Curriculum*. London: Routledge.

Hillman, M., Adams, J. and Whitelegg, J. (2000) *One False Move: A Study of Children's Independent Mobility*. London: Policy Studies Institute.

Hutt, S.J., Tyler, S., Hutt, C. and Christopherson, H. (1989) *Play, Exploration and Learning*. London: Routledge.

Lambirth, A. and Goouch, K. (2006) 'Golden times of writing: the creative compliance of writing journals'. *Literacy*, 40: 146–52.

Layard, R. and Dunn, J. (2009) *A Good Childhood. Searching for Values in a Competitive Age*. London: Penguin.

Malaguzzi, L. (2004) 'Walking on threads of silk'. *Children in Europe*, 6: 10–15.
Martin, P. (2005) *Making Happy People*. London: Fourth Estate.
Nias, J. (1989) *Primary Teachers Talking: A Study of Teaching as Work*. London: Routledge.
Nutbrown, C. (2006) *Key Concepts in Early Childhood Education and Care*. London: Sage.
OECD (2001) *Starting Strong I*. Paris: Organisation for Economic Co-operation and Development.
——(2006) *Starting Strong II*. Paris: OECD.
Office of National Statistics (2001) *The 2001 Census*. London: ONS.
Papatheodorou, T. and Moyles, J. (eds) (2009) *Learning Together in the Early Years*. London: Routledge.
Piaget, J. (1959) *The Language and Thought of the Child*. London: Routledge and Kegan Paul Ltd.
Powell, S. (2008) 'The value of play: constructions of play in England's national policies'. *Children and Society*, 23: 29–42.
Sachs, J. (2003) *Teacher Activism: Mobilising the Profession*. Nottingham: British Educational Research Association.
Siraj-Blatchford, I., Sylva, K., Muttock, S., Gilden, R. and Bell, D. (2002) *Researching Effective Pedagogy in the Early Years*. London: Department for Education and Skills. Research Report 356.
Strandell, H. (2000) 'What is the use of children's play: preparation or social participation?' In H.Penn (ed) *Early Childhood Services: Theory, Policy and Practice*. Buckingham: Open University Press.
Sylva, K., Melhuish, E., Sammons, P., Siraj-Blatchford, I. and Taggart, B. (2004) *The Effective Provision of Pre-school Education Project*. London: University of London Institute of Education.
The Guardian (2008) 'Playing for keeps'. Wednesday 9 April 2008. www.guardian.co.uk/society/2008/apr/09/children.play.strategy [accessed 18 September 2009].
Trevarthen, C. (1998) 'The child's need to learn a culture'. In M. Woodhead, D. Faulkner and K. Littleton (eds) *Cultural Worlds of Early Childhood*. London: Routledge/ Open University.
United Nations (1989) *Convention on the Rights of the Child*. New York: UN.
Wall, K. (2006) *Special Needs and Early Years*. London: PCP/Sage.
Wertsch, J. V. (1991) *Voices of the Mind, A Sociocultural Approach to Mediated Action*. Cambridge, M.A.: Harvard University Press.
Wood, E. (2007) 'New directions in play: consensus or collision?' *Education* 3–13, 35: 309–22.
Woodhead, M. (2005) 'Early childhood development: a question of rights'. *International Journal of Early Childhood*, 37(3): 79–98.

Chapter 6

The importance of mixed age groups in Cameroon

Bame Nsamenang[1]

Introduction

Peer culture is central to supporting African children's learning and development of norms. However, it has not been well analyzed or researched and remains a largely uncharted developmental niche. This chapter examines parent–child relationships, child-to-child sociability and how both interact with each other in the family traditions and peer cultures in sub-Saharan Africa in general and Cameroon in particular. Interpersonal relationships and social interactions presuppose social development; they constitute the social fields in which the dynamics of individual development and identity formation play out. The chapter depicts a context of social development wherein the centrality of the family and mixed-aged peer groups is evident and where traditionally parents have not retained the sole responsibility to care for and manage children; rather they delegate several aspects of social protection and care to older siblings, who are 'better together' in peer learning cultures. The chapter also discusses how the respective roles of children, parents, other adults and peers in social development have been transformed and reconfigured by changing circumstances such as the increasing number of children attending formal schooling in institutions and migration to urban areas and out of Cameroon. It also reveals the process of developing a sense of self as the dynamic connection of individual personal identity to a changing social identity (Woodhead 2008), as a function of a given child's group affiliations at various stages of development. This genre of relational individuation in Cameroon, as in much of Africa, does not leave out 'individuality', that sense of personal identity, which collectivism research so far has largely trivialized or failed to track in African children (Nsamenang 2008a).

My account draws on field research (e.g. Nsamenang and Lamb 1995) with the Nso of western Cameroon, and on selected relevant literature in anthropology and psychology about other African peoples (e.g. Jahoda 1982; Serpell 1993; Zimba 2002). The Nso ethnic community constitutes the largest fondom (kingdom) in the North West Region of Cameroon. According to Nsamenang and Lamb (1995), the vast majority of the Nso population lives in their ancestral land in Bui Division, but some have migrated and settled elsewhere throughout Cameroon and abroad. The majority of immigrants in one geographical locale are settled 65 miles (about 108 km) to the south in Bamenda, the Regional capital and base for my research. Whether they are in their ancestral land or in the diaspora, intracultural variation is perceptible among the Nso in parental values by virtue of sex, generation, rural–urban residence, religion (African, Christianity or Islam) and educational level (Nsamenang and Lamb 1995). Nevertheless, considerable similarities persist from a pronatalist and theocentric theory of the universe, the value of children, and the accreditation of children in 'hands-on processes such as being responsible, being aware, and motivated engagement' in familial and communal affairs from an early age (Nsamenang 2008a: 211).

The ecology of childhood in Cameroon

Children are born into contexts, defined by a physical setting, a social system and traditions of practice that structure and give meaning to the ecology and its affordances. To narrow the full range of environmental factors that impinge on child development in general and social development in particular in Cameroon, I have organized them within the three components of the developmental niche offered by Super and Harkness (1986), namely, the physical and social settings of childhood, culturally regulated customs and practices of childcare and childrearing, and the psychology of caretakers and teachers.

The physical setting

Cameroon lies less than 5 degrees north of the equator on the West African Coast. This triangle-shaped country occupies an area of under 190,000 square miles and its vegetation ranges from a dense tropical forest in the coastal south through savanna in the midlands to a dry Sahel in the far north. Food geography, that is, which foods are staples in which vegetative zone, is a key determinant of agrarian livelihoods in which both boys and girls, from an early age, are actively engaged, each according to perceived ability.

Cameroon has substantial wealth, derived from abundance of agricultural, human and mineral resources. Yet, it cannot garner the means for effective social security provisions and even basic health care services for its vast child population. Pence and Nsamenang (2008: 33) claim such resources have 'been drained by and for foreign interests', with only pittances of huge profits repatriated as donor charities to indigent Cameroon.

The social ecology

Cameroon's estimated population of 18.5 million people represents a mix of Christian, Muslim and indigenous religious groups. Some of its 239 linguistically distinct ethnic groups (Che 1985) trace their ancestral roots to different ends of the continent and beyond. The social ecology of Nso childhood, as an exemplar, reveals that a child is likely to have other siblings and not only parents as social partners (Nsamenang 2008a). Even the only child in a family would not be alone but would have peer visitors or residential relatives and friends as regular or frequent peer partners. The Nso child is typically a member of a large family, including an average of 4.7 siblings per family in the Bamenda highlands of Cameroon (Nsamenang 1992a), which compares with a fertility of 5.15 in Nigeria (National Population Commission, 2000) and Ware's (1983) report of a regional fertility range of 4.5 siblings per family for Cameroon and 7.0 for most West African countries. When we take into consideration the extended family members and its child and youth cohorts, we can visualize the scope of the social interactive range of a Cameroonian child.

The psychology of caregivers and teachers

The psychology of caretakers and teachers refers to the ethnotheories that give (directive) focus to childrearing values and practices (Nsamenang and Lamb 1995). For example, a holistic and theocentric theory of the universe promotes positive reproductive attitudes in Cameroon (Nsamenang *et al.* 2008), implying 'the desire for and high valuation of children' (Nsamenang 1992a: 129). The foundational idea of caregiving psychology in Cameroon, as with the Samburu and Turkana of Kenya, is the position that the 'root of humanity is children' (Lanyasunya and Lesolayia 2001: 7).

The Nso metaphor for child is botanical; it is *seed*, nursed into a seedling and cultivated into fruition in a *sociological garden* (Nsamenang 2002) in which roles are shared among multi-age gardeners of mixed abilities and statuses. Nso parents prepare their next generations not from a positioning of children being born without the knowledge and skills with which to make sense of and cope with the world, but from keen awareness of a maturational ability in children to grow into or learn the knowledge and skills they need and that are needed today (Nsamenang 2008b). This belief is illustrated in parenting programmes that assign livelihood tasks to children such as running errands for parents and elder siblings and doing household chores. By doing so the children are disposed to acquire and transmit culture or create and modify their cultural curricula. As accredited novice-gardeners, children systematically learn or teach themselves some knowledge and skills as well as some of the requirements of the globalized world. The task and role of being a novice-gardener today is complicated by the coexistence in the same families and communities of three heritages (Mazrui 1986) of the traditions of early childhood development care and education (Pence and Nsamenang 2008) from three significant sources, viz, African, Islamic-Arabic, and Western-Christian civilizations.

Mixed-age groups in rural and urban communities

The care and protection of the next generations, particularly during the early years of life directly involves the cultural worlds of communities and their offspring. In Cameroon, as in much of Africa, childcare and education is a collective enterprise rather than a parental prerogative (Nsamenang 1992b), in which parents and kin, including siblings, are active participants. Most Cameroonian mothers exclusively breastfed zero to six-month-old babies, and today some mothers are still assisted by permanent live-in relatives or babysitters, most of them girls but sometimes boys between 11 and 15 years of age; they provided and to a limited extent still offer the care of babies aged 6–24 months. The usual practice was and still is for a prepubescent female or male relative or family friend to start hands-on training in home care and child tending chores pending childbirth. From an early age, siblings observed and participated in graduated family tasks and caregiving to younger siblings.

> Once children become members of the peer group, they must carve out their own niche in terms of secure and reliable friends from whom to abstract appropriate rule systems and a sense of security. As children and adolescents keep together, older ones begin to 'boss' the young, acting as *father* or *mother*.
>
> (Nsamenang 2002: 77)

This pattern of early learning through caregiving is rooted in an African belief and 'investment' in children's developmental, participatory learning. African cultures in general and the Nso of Cameroon in particular separate the learning of childhood skills from the life stage of parenthood. Accordingly, the Nso position sibling caregiving as developmental learning (Nsamenang 2008a) that children learn and enact as part of the 'shared management, caretaking, and socially distributed support' of the family (Weisner 1997: 23). Childcare and child protection are not an adult or parental privilege. This contrasts with Euro-Western cultures that position childcare as a specialized task of adulthood. That is, African children are not only 'certified' partners in caregiving and child protection but also significant contributors to family and community life. However, 'peer caregiving is more widespread in villages (rural communities) than in towns because parents consider most city neighborhoods too unsafe' to leave their child with other children (Nsamenang 1992a: 151).

Since most children now avail themselves of education in organized settings such as schools, relatives and sibling caregivers are no longer readily available, though adolescent babysitters are still used in more complex childcare arrangements in urban settings. 'The Nigerian urban working mother', like her Cameroonian equivalent, 'is able to play the dual roles of being a mother and an employee successfully due to the availability of childcare services such as homemaids, nannies, day care centres, nursery schools and kindergarten' (Ogbimi and Alao 1998: 48). Although institutional daycare and preschools have become popular, more so in urban settings than rural communities, this is not so much because daycare centres or preschools truly promote early childhood development, but more so because they play custodial roles for busy mothers (Ogbimi and Alao 1998). The increase in school attendance has not entirely eliminated sibling caregiving or other peer group activities, such as domestic chores and street trading, but it has somehow modified the childhood routines (Bekombo 1981). Pupils and students of all ages and sex at different levels of education can still be seen functioning in the family economy and reciprocal sociability of peer networks, for various purposes in educational institutions.

The role of parents and peer mentors

The previous section illustrates how indigenous African early childhood education has been wedged into the familial and communal spheres to socialize responsible intelligence through the child's active participation in acceptable and valued familial and economic activities (Nsamenang 2006). Parents can influence the nature of sibling relationships, both through direct guidance and indirectly through the types of relationships that they form with each other and with each of their children. Next to parents, one of the strongest but largely underexplored influences in a child's development is her or his siblings. Tacit African theories posit children's innate capacity to be agents of their own developmental learning in multi-age peer groups in which parental values and actions prime responsible intelligences by permitting older children to serve as peer mentors. Most parents are 'only partially available to guide and supervise child baby-sitting and sibling caretaking' (Nsamenang 1992b: 432). Much of children's contribution to sibling caregiving, 'peerhood' work and self-learning occurs primarily through social exchanges and distributive norms in different social sectors and activity settings in which the young engage with significant others such as parents, caregivers, teachers and peers. As a result, most children in rural settings and urban slums in Cameroon spend more time in peer groups than with parents or other adults. This explains why socialization is organized 'such that children can acquire physical, intellectual, and practical education through their own initiatives' and efforts (Nsamenang and Lamb 1995: 622).

Sibling relations are, in and of themselves, important as siblings and peers relate to one another and influence the social and 'productive' world in which they play and develop. The psychosocial skills that children gain through peer group interactions and sociability are also useful in lifespan perspective in a wide range of lifespan circumstances. In my understanding and experience in Cameroon, especially among the Nso of western Cameroon, 'peerhood' extends beyond friendship, to include among others: (1) friendship within a wider 'comradeship' or a sense and experience of being 'better together' even as non-friends or enemies in the same peer 'gang'; (2) friendship/enmity/deference to older or more 'forceful' peers is transient but de facto status ordering seems 'stable'; (3) age-grading is lifelong and reminiscences of the earliest companionships and enmities are with little or no rancor, although this is changing rather rapidly. Conflict is bound to arise within peer cultures, however. 'Both conflict and friendliness between siblings help children to learn to consider other people's feelings, needs, and beliefs. Both kinds of behaviour may be necessary to give children a variety of experiences in learning to deal with others' (Chiakem 2009: 29). Children 'transform confusions and ambiguities from the adult world into the familiar routines of peer culture' (Corsaro 1990: 12). 'Thus, children are not merely active accommodators but are also creative social producers of their own worlds' (Nsamenang and Lamb 1995: 624).

The role of parents and peer mentors is three-fold (Nsamenang 2002): (1) to guide children to understand and accept the appropriate adult identity and models toward which they are being socialized; (2) to communicate standards of valued behavior and virtue; and (3) to prime or sensitize children to acceptable rule systems and standards and ensure their acquisition. Ethnic communities in Cameroon, as in much of West Africa, see children in their maturational unfolding:

> not as a set of organisms to be molded into a pattern of behavior specified in advance as educational outcomes, but as newcomers to a community of practice,

> for whom the desirable outcome of a period of apprenticeship is that they would appropriate the system of meanings that informs the community's practices.
>
> (Serpell 2008: 74)

Accordingly, the parents' didactic involvement in children's learning generally is minimal and peripheral, even distant. The parents' role is nonetheless critical in that parental values and expectations filter into and pervade the peer culture, exerting a directive, regulatory force on children, even when the parents are not available. This is possible because the 'liberal' values of parents, 'whose direct intervention is no longer needed', bind and direct children (Zempleni-Rabain 1979) and their elder mentors to spend more time within the freedom and self-regulation of the peer culture than with parents (Nsamenang and Lamb 1995; Pence and Nsamenang 2008). In doing so, children 'graduate' from one role-setting and participative sphere to another, steadily maturing toward adulthood. The boys and girls who are poised for the responsibility of adult life are evaluated as proficient on the basis of their social, moral, intellectual and practical prowess within the peer culture (Cameroon 1981) rather than with a score of intellectual or cognitive readiness and speed (Serpell 1993).

Learning in mixed-aged peer groups

To train for responsibility, parents, older siblings and peer mentors allocate to children caregiving duties (Chiakem 2009), chores (Nsamenang 1992b) and send them on errands (Ogunaike and Houser 2002). Children in Cameroon perform 'a much wider range of economically productive and maintenance activities than is the case' in most other societies (Nsamenang 2001: 7298). Such 'child work' is real-life duties and not non-essential tasks such as pretend-play, because the welfare of the family depends on children performing them effectively. For example, if a child is sent to fetch or purchase a food item at a neighborhood store for a family meal, this has to be properly executed. See Figures 6.1 and 6.2.

It has been suggested that children are 'better together' (Rogoff 2003) within the free spirit and self-regulation of the peer culture; they interstimulate and mentor each other, disagree and defer to more forceful and competent peers. A balance of friendliness and conflict in the peer group can provide a unique opportunity for children to develop social and behavioral skills in their own terms that will enable them to manage anger and disagreements and to offer help and comfort to others. Learning these skills in the peer culture prepares children to adjust to the social demands of school and out-of-school life.

In a typical peer-group scenario, multi-age, multi-sex, groups of children ranging in age from twenty months to six or seven years could be found in the rural neighborhood or urban slum with one or two regular caretakers of eight to ten years of age, who keep an eye over the younger children as regular mentors and supervisors. The authority of elder siblings over younger ones derives from that of parents over children. With such delegated authority, older siblings are charged with the care and supervision of younger ones, whom they can reprimand and correct (Nsamenang

Figure 6.1 Participative learning 1
Source: Copyright A. Bame Nsamenang

1992b). Thus, peer mentors guide, control and discipline younger ones and peers. Adults respond to non-conforming children by inducing guilt, shame or depriving them of certain privileges or cherished items such as food and by disciplining them. When children engage in behaviors that are contrary to parental expectations and rules, peer mentors and elder siblings also make them feel guilty and to experience shame. The peer culture extends and brings into children's discourses familial issues and processes that are basic to identity formation. The image of identity development in African cultures emphasizes the shared and social, rather than the unique and individual, aspects of identity (Nsamenang 2008a). See Figures 6.3 and 6.4.

Figure 6.2 Participative learning 2
Source: Copyright A. Bame Nsamenang

Figure 6.3 Helping with household chores 1
Source: Copyright A. Bame Nsamenang

Figure 6.4 Helping with household chores 2
Source: Copyright A. Bame Nsamenang

While Vygotsky (1978) is embraced in the West for his development of self through social processes, in some way traditional African cultures transcend Vygotsky by sensitizing children from an early age to seek out others, to extract 'intelligences' (Nsamenang 2006), and to define self more so in peer groups than in adult–child networks, such that children can 'gain significance from and through their relationships with others' (Ellis 1978: 6). In a country where the majority of children have become more knowledgeable about a globalized world than their parents, the child-to-child template requires discovery and incorporation into early childhood development and schooling policies and programmes.

Changing peer cultures in Cameroon

No human community is ecologically or culturally homogeneous. As noted earlier, Cameroon is a truly diversified country. The diversity derives from the colonial legacies of European imperialists, Islamic-Arabic influences and the cultural traditions of over 239 ethnic communities (Che 1985). The stratification systems of Cameroon today, as with those of Africa, are a mixture of traditional patterns and new developments (Peil 1977). As in most contexts and cultures, children's lives in Cameroon are undergoing rapid change affecting the quality of children's connections with their environment, siblings and peers. As many of the skills needed for functional citizenship are learned within the context of institutional education, most children are no longer assigned to a life work and trained by parents or mentors. Some parents even attend school. Additionally, many children in Cameroon – especially middle-class and urban children – seem to have less time for unstructured play as they are compelled to balance a flurry of parent-organized tasks and teacher-planned activities. In previous times, children's experience of 'place' in rural areas and urban slums involved time they spent alone, or with peers, exploring their environment. In addition, rural and low-income families tend to encourage different skills and experiences than middle-class families do or did. Working-class parents tended to give their children greater freedom to manipulate their physical environments to create their own play opportunities, while middle-class parents created more controlled landscapes for play – close to their homes – with manufactured play items, such as swing sets, sandboxes and toys.

Concluding points and emerging issues in research

Schisms and dilemmas in the childcare and education landscape of Cameroon are evident in a number of areas: the scarcity of the traditional support of childcare, especially sibling caregiving, and the fact that children today are spending less time in peer groups outside their homes and are relying more on their parents and technology for guiding the kinds of creative play children of previous generations fostered among themselves at various stages of life in peer cultures. A further issue of concern is the fate of non-Western systems of early years care and education in Cameroon, which has been similar elsewhere in Africa. In spite of their ubiquity throughout Africa, indigenous African and Islamic-Arabic patterns of care and education are a 'submerged system'. Despite their successful operation from antiquity, they remain relatively unknown to development planners and therefore are seldom taken into explicit account in their policy development and programmatic models, which are typically Eurocentric (World Bank 1999: 1). In 1990 the World Bank recorded over 40,000 Koranic schools in Niger alone, yet these schools 'have not been considered as schools at all' (World Bank 1999: 2); neither are they considered part of the school system in Cameroon.

Although Euro-Western evidence acknowledges vibrant diversity in early child development realities, the current understandings do not yet 'mirror the immense variation in global developmental trajectories and cultural curricula that generate them' (Nsamenang 2009: 23) in the theory, research, intervention and pedagogy of international psychology (Stevens and Gielen 2007). By placing an excessive emphasis on externally provided, standalone early childhood development services or psychosocial support of children, we are in danger of discounting the importance of everyday love, support and social capital that children receive from families and communities, even from child-headed families (Richter *et al.* 2006).

If institutional public early childhood development programmes and services are appropriately advocated as 'a good start' for children aged zero to eight years, they should incorporate the participative spirit, child-to-child sociability and self-generation of peer cultures, such as described in this chapter. The way forward is to raise children who understand and appreciate multiple worlds, through young scholars that frame their own contextually sensitive research questions, and through gatekeepers who appreciate the riches of the past, as much as the possibilities of the future (Pence and Nsamenang 2008).

Point for reflection and discussion

Nsamenang argues that mixed-age peer groups are central to supporting African children's learning. How are parent–child relationships and child-to-child sociability related in the processes of caretaking and of transmission of family values, routines and traditions? What is the value of peer culture in the development of social and personal identities? What can we learn from this tradition of upbringing in the context of urban environments?

Note

1 Bame Nsamenang's research interests are early childhood and youth development in context and Africa-sensitive teacher education textbook development. He is professor of psychology and learning science at the School of Education of the University of Yaoundé, Cameroon. He also directs the Human Development Resource Centre, a research and service facility.

References

Bekombo, M. (1981) 'The child in Africa: socialization, education and work'. In G. Rodgers and G. Standing (eds) *Child Work, Poverty and Underdevelopment*. Geneva: International Labour Organization.

Cameroon (1981) *Encyclopedie de la Republique Unie du Cameroun [Encyclopedia of the United Republic of Cameroon]*, Douala, Cameroon: Eddy Ness.

Che, M. (1985) 'Seminar on language: proposes "Fulfulde, Beti, Duala" for Cameroon'. *Cameroon Tribune*, 587: 4.

Chiakem, O. (2009) 'The role of sibling caretakers in the development of social abilities of younger siblings'. Unpublished thesis. University of Buea, Cameroon.

Corsaro, W.A. (1990) 'The underlife of nursery school: young children's social representations of adult roles'. In G. Duven and B. Lloyd (eds) *Social Representation and the Development of Knowledge*. Cambridge: Cambridge University Press.

Ellis, J. (1978) *West African Families in Great Britain*. London: Routledge.

Jahoda, G. (1982) *Psychology and Anthropology*. London, UK: Academic Press.

Lanyasunya, A.R. and Lesolayia, M.S. (2001) 'El-barta child and family project'. Working Papers in Early Childhood Development, No. 28. The Hague, The Netherlands: Bernard van Leer Foundation.

Mazrui, A.A. (1986) *The Africans*. New York, USA: Praeger.

National Population Commission (2000) *Nigeria Demographic and Health Survey 1999*. Abuja, Nigeria: National Population Commission.

Nsamenang, A.B. (1992a) *Human Development in Cultural Context: A Third World Perspective*. Newbury Park, C.A.: Sage.

——(1992b) 'Early childhood care and education in Cameroon'. In M.E. Lamb *et al.* (eds) *Day Care in Context: Socio-Cultural Perspectives*. Hillsdale, N.J.: Erlbaum.

——(2001) 'Indigenous view on human development: a West African perspective'. In Neil J. Smelser and Paul B. Baltes (eds) *International Encyclopedia of the Social and Behavioral Sciences*. London: Elsevier, pp. 7297–99

——(2002) 'Adolescence in sub-Saharan Africa: an image constructed from Africa's triple inheritance'. In B.B. Brown, R.W. Larson and T.S. Saraswathi (eds) *The World's Youth: Adolescence in Eight Regions of the Globe*. London: Cambridge University Press.

——(2006) 'Human ontogenesis: an indigenous African view on development and intelligence'. *International Journal of Psychology*, 41: 293–7.

——(2008a) 'Agency in early childhood learning and development in Cameroon'. *Contemporary Issues in Early Childhood*, 9: 211–23.

——(2008b) '(Mis)understanding ECD in Africa: the force of local and global motives'. In M. Garcia, A. Pence and J. Evans (eds) *Africa's Future – Africa's Challenge: Early Childhood Care and Development in Sub-Saharan Africa*. Washington D.C.: World Bank.

——(2009) 'Cultures in early childhood care and education'. In M. Fleer, M. Hedegaard and J. Trudge (eds) *World Yearbook of Education: Childhood Studies and the Impact of Globalization: Policies and Practices at Global and Local Levels*. New York: Routledge.

Nsamenang, A.B. and Lamb, M.E. (1995) 'The force of beliefs: how the parental values of the Nso of Northwest Cameroon shape children's progress towards adult models'. *Journal of Applied Developmental Psychology*, 16: 613–27.

Nsamenang, A.B., Fai, P.J., Ngoran, G.N. *et al.* (2008) 'Ethnotheories of developmental learning in the Western Grassfields of Cameroon'. In P.R. Dasen and A. Akkari (eds) *Educational Theories and Practices from the 'Majority World'*. New Delhi, India: Sage.

Ogbimi, G.E. and Alao, J.A. (1998) 'Developing sustainable day care services in rural communities of Nigeria'. *Early Child Development and Care*, 145: 47–58.

Ogunaike, O.A. and Houser, Jr., R.F. (2002) 'Yoruba toddler's engagement in errands and cognitive performance on the Yoruba Mental Subscale'. *International Journal of Behavioral Development*, 26: 145–53.

Peil, M. (1977) *Consensus and Conflict in African Societies*. London: Longman.

Pence, A.R. and Nsamenang, A.B. (2008) *A case for ECD in sub-saharan Africa*. Working Paper on Early Childhood Development, No. 51. The Hague, The Netherlands: Bernard van Leer Foundation.

Richter, L., Foster, G. and Sherr, L. (2006) *Where the heart is: meeting the psychosocial needs of young children in the context of HIV/AIDS*. The Hague, The Netherlands: Bernard van Leer Foundation.

Rogoff, B. (2003) *The Cultural Nature of Human Development*. Oxford: Oxford University Press.

Serpell, R. (1993) *The Significance of Schooling: Life-Journeys into an African Society*. Cambridge: Cambridge University Press.

——(2008) 'Participatory appropriation and the cultivation of nurturance: A case study of African primary school health science curriculum development'. In P.R. Dasen and A. Akkari (eds) *Educational Theories and Practices from the 'Majority World'*. New Delhi, India: Sage.

Super, C.M. and Harkness, S. (1986) 'The developmental niche: a conceptualization at the interface of child and culture'. *International Journal of Behavioral Development*, 9: 545–69.

Stevens, M.J. and Gielen, U.P. (2007) *Toward a Global Psychology: Theory, Research, Intervention, and Pedagogy*. Mahwah, N.J.: Lawrence Erlbaum Associates, Inc.

Vygotsky, L. (1978) *Mind in Society: The Development of Higher Psychological Processes*. Cambridge, M.S.: Cambridge University Press.

Ware, H. (1983) 'Male and female life cycles'. In C. Oppong (ed) *Male and Female in West Africa*. London: Allen & Unwin, pp. 6–31.

Weisner, T.S. (1997) 'Support for children and the African family crisis'. In T.S. Weisner, C. Bradley and C.P. Kilbride (eds) *African Families and the Crisis of Social Change*. Westport, C.T.: Bergin and Garvey.

World Bank. (1999) 'Education and Koranic literacy in West Africa', *IK Notes*, 11: 1–4.

Woodhead, M. (2008) 'Identity at birth – and identity in development?'. In M. Woodhead and L. Brooker (eds) *Early Childhood in Focus 3: Developing Positive Identities, Diversity and Young Children*. Milton Keynes, UK: The Open University.

Zempleni-Rabain, J. (1979) 'Food and strategy involved in learning fraternal external exchange among Wolof children'. In P. Alexander (ed) *French Perspectives in African Studies*. London: Oxford University Press.

Zimba, R.F. (2002) 'Indigenous conceptions of childhood development and social realities in southern Africa'. In H. Keller, Y.P. Poortinga and A. Scholmerish (eds) *Between Cultures and Biology: Perspectives on Ontogenetic Development*. Cambridge: Cambridge University Press.

Chapter 7

Peer relations in Brazilian daycare centres

A new focus for early childhood education

Maria Clotilde Rossetti-Ferreira, Zilma de Moraes, Ramos de Oliveira, Mara Ignez Campos-de-Carvalho and Katia Souza Amorim[1]

Introduction

One of the most challenging tasks we face nowadays in Brazil is to transform the views that adults have about early peer interaction into new perspectives that are just beginning to be spread among daycare teachers. The pedagogical point of view of many teachers is still centred on the adult, i.e. on the transmission of an already made culture, with the concern to control and introduce discipline quite early on in young children's lives. In many ways, this adult-centred perspective mirrors teachers' own experiences, since their own education has been based on an authoritarian teaching model. For many researchers, barriers against pedagogical work centred on children's needs has been influenced by the historical construction of children attending daycare centres and pre-schools in the 19th and early 20th century as recipients of charity bestowed on the socially handicapped/deprived (Kulhman 1991). Following the two World Wars and the battle for human rights, the plea for the right to education for children of diverse social groups was extended to children attending early years services. However, that concern was suppressed during the military dictatorship, which governed Brazil with exceptional powers from 1964 until the 1980s. The principle of early child education and care as a right for the children, an option for families and an obligation of the State was only introduced with the re-democratization of Brazil and the new Constitution of 1988 (Brasil 1988).

Since then, an intense process of transformation of early education and care has been occurring. This has been influenced by changes in family structure and roles, as well as a widespread social movement that has been striving to include early childhood care and education in the educational system. Those changes are much needed in Brazil, where there is a large gap between those who have a very high standard of life and a majority who fight for their survival. Schools and particularly early childhood care and education settings, in partnership with families, are slowly changing and beginning to promote a more balanced access to knowledge. Through these initiatives, it is intended to make developmental opportunities available to all citizens, by providing them with significant experiences that may enlarge and enrich their cultural repertoire, and support the construction of their personal and family identity.

Consequently, in Brazil, the traditional philanthropic rationale, which heretofore has guided the elaboration of many early childhood care and education pedagogical proposals, is gradually being replaced by new parameters, documents, policies and practices. However, the replacement of the old guidelines with new ways of thinking and working has created various challenges for the planning of pedagogical practices in childcare centres and for the training of practitioners. These difficulties are particularly apparent in public and philanthropic services all over the country, which are attended by children from low-income families. In these settings the training and working conditions of the staff are often precarious and the adult–child ratio is very low.

In the remainder of the chapter we discuss a number of related research studies conducted by the Brazilian Investigation Centre on Human Development and Early Childhood Education (CINDEDI) at the University of São Paulo, Campus of Ribeirão Preto. The results of these studies have served to support practitioners to provide enhanced opportunities for the children in their care.

The construction of a new perspective on early child development and education for group settings

A socio-historical perspective on human development, supported on Vygotsky's (1978, 1986) and Wallon's (1942) works, has become the major theoretical influence guiding the discussion of early childhood education and care curricula in Brazil today. Through it, young children's development is understood as a process that is constructed through the interactions children establish with diverse partners in concrete social situations, which are organized by adults according to their conceptions about child development and the ways to promote it. These intrinsic relations between children's development and context are guaranteed by the fact that the immaturity of human babies obliges them to be dependent for a long period on a more experienced partner, usually an adult, who can help them to satisfy their basic needs and so guarantee their survival. Such an intimate relation is enhanced by the human baby's facial and body expressivity and innate perceptual and response organization. These favour arousal and readiness to perceive and respond to human characteristics such as facial features and rhythms. This supports the establishment of a jointly constructed communication system that favours the construction of adult–baby affective bonds.

In Brazilian culture, the mother is usually understood as the main partner in such an adult–baby bond. She has the interpretational resources for attributing certain meanings to the baby's diffuse movements. These are based on representations constructed during her personal life in specific socio-cultural contexts. The baby's movements provide communication cues that suggest some joint course of action. In her response, the mother provides specific meanings for the situation in which both she and the baby are involved. In doing so, she interprets the baby for the surrounding world, and the world for the baby (Lyra and Rossetti-Ferreira 1995).

However, by prioritizing the mother's role and the traditional childrearing focus, which usually excludes the father and other interactional partners, early childhood education and care practice in group settings was somehow being distorted. This was initially observed by the CINDEDI research group in their studies of childcare centres conducted during the 1970s and 1980s. It was demonstrated that, in those environments, the care model provided by a mother in a nuclear family was clearly inadequate in the context of the childcare centres studied, and probably in any group setting for young children. One can imagine the helplessness of a mother with quintuplets, considered an adequate adult:child ratio in a baby group under the responsibility of one caregiver. Furthermore, the researchers observed that the emphasis on special attention and stimulation of each individual child, 'as you would do with your own children at home', resulted in stress for the caregivers and in long waiting times for passive children with nothing to do, in empty and non-stimulating environments (Rossetti-Ferreira 1988).

It became clear to the members of the research group that group settings for young children differed from the family environment and required new skills and knowledge, which were distinct from mother substitute care. In essence, in childcare centres a caregiver does not necessarily have an exclusive affectionate bond with each child. The caregiver shares with the families the care and education of their children, and structures the environment and the routines for more autonomous activities of several young children (Campos-de-Carvalho and Rossetti-Ferreira 1993). This strategy allows the caregiver to provide attention to individual children when needed.

These initial studies of Brazilian childcare centres during the 1970s also indicated that the low quality of early childhood education and care, characterized by low adult:child ratios and distorted practices, was exacerbated by poorly organized and resourced physical environments. This led to passivity in the children and hindered early peer interactions (Secaf-Silveira *et al.* 1987).

Spatial arrangements in childcare centres

Different ways of organizing the space can lead to a wide diversity of social behaviours. This is particularly the case in group settings for young children, such as childcare centres, where the caregiver is usually responsible for many children and where the partners most available for interaction are other children. Peer interaction is as important as child–adult interaction for child development (Hartup 1996). Thus questions can be raised regarding the ways an environment can promote or hinder those interactions among young children in childcare centres. The younger the child, the more the spatial organization supports their activities and interactions (Olds 1987).

In his studies with two- to three-year-old children in French childcare centres, Legendre (1989) had already shown that a structured spatial organization clearly favoured peer interaction even in environments where there were many toys and furniture available. Using Legendre's studies as a starting point, we studied the relation between spatial arrangement – the way furniture and equipment are distributed and positioned in relation to each other – and the use of space by groups of young children in childcare centres. We began our studies in Brazilian childcare centres with groups of two- to three-year-old children and their caregivers in two philanthropic and one university childcare centres (Campos-de-Carvalho and Rossetti-Ferreira 1993; Campos-de-Carvalho and Mingorance 1999). More recently we have extended the analysis to groups of one- to two-year-old children and three- to four-year-old children in municipal childcare centres (Bomfim and Campos-de-Carvalho 2002; Bomfim and Campos-de-Carvalho 2006).

Data were recorded with photographic (initial studies) or video cameras, during free activities, in three conditions: (1) Phase I – usual empty space, without circumscribed zones, defined as areas delimited at least on three sides by barriers, like furniture, walls, a difference in ground level, etc.; (2) Phase II – that same space was surrounded by low shelves (1.10 x 0.30 x 0.50 m), which were needed as there was not any other furniture to delimit the circumscribed zones at the next phase; (3) Phase III – two or three circumscribed zones organized with little shelves, which delimited two sides, and using, whenever possible, a corner of the playroom to delimit the two other sides, keeping a small opening for children to get in out. To determine the location of each child and caregiver a plan of the playroom with the area divided into 1 m^2 was used. Specific areas of the room were delimited and the children's preference for certain areas simultaneously available in the playroom was analyzed, using a behavioural mapping technique (Proshansky *et al.* 1970).

Here, we present a summarized account of the main results obtained in our studies, comparing different age groups, giving special attention to the support offered by spatial arrangement for the use of space (see detailed descriptions of the method and results in Bomfim and Campos-de-Carvalho 2006; Campos-de-Carvalho 2004; Campos-de-Carvalho and Rossetti-Ferreira 1993). Figure 7.1 presents, as an example, children's spatial distribution for different age groups, during the spatial arrangement with two circumscribed zones – each point indicates one per cent of use of each square, considering all children's positions recorded in it and taking all positions recorded in the phase at 100 per cent.

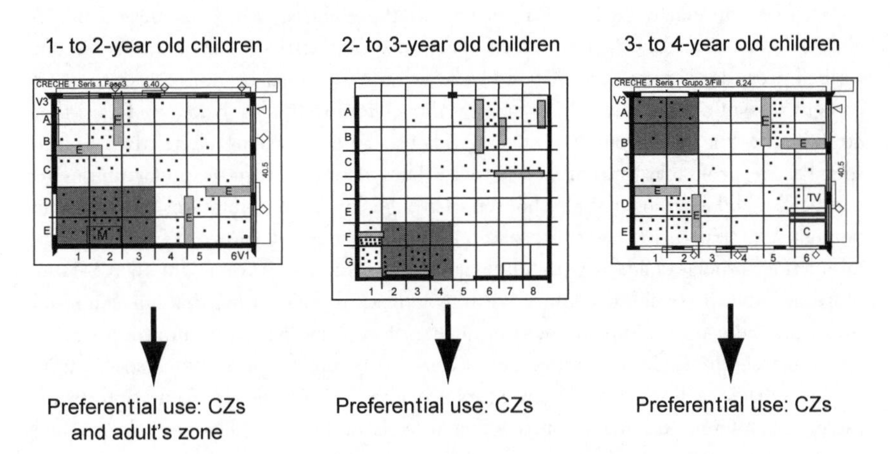

Figure 7.1 Children's distribution during the spatial arrangement with two circumscribed zones (CZs) in three age groups. Each point indicates one per cent of use of each square (1 m2); shaded or hatched areas indicate the space surrounding the adult's most frequent locations; smaller rectangles indicate the location of the shelves.

Source: Copyright Mara Campos-de-Carvalho

The analysis showed that children aged three to four years displayed a pattern of space use similar to the one observed with Brazilian and French children aged two to three years: (a) in the usual arrangement, without circumscribed zones, there was a preferential use of the area around the caregiver, named the adult's zone – but there were few occurrences of interaction with the caregiver and among children; (b) when the shelves were introduced, still without circumscribed zones, a preferential use of space around the shelves was observed; (c) in arrangements with circumscribed zones, such zones were preferentially used, favouring peer interaction.

Children aged one to two years, however, showed a different pattern of behaviour in arrangements with circumscribed zones: they spent a similar time in those zones as in the adult's zone. This indicates that, when compared with the two older groups, one- to two-year-old children look for more proximity to the caregiver, in any type of spatial arrangement, although some proximity to other children was also observed. This points to the role of the caregiver as an attachment figure at the daycare centre, chiefly at this early age. Similar age trends were shown in a study by Rossetti-Ferreira *et al.* 1985, when 15-, 21-, 27-, 33- and 39-month-old groups of four first-born English children were observed with a caregiver and in the presence or the brief absence of their mothers. There was a clear age increase of peer interaction in all periods (before, during and after a five-minute separation from the mother). The 15- and 21-month-old children showed the lowest proportions of peer interactions as compared with their interactions with an adult (mother and/or caregiver), while the 33- and 39-month-old children presented larger proportions of peer interaction.

Our results point out that opportunities for early peer interactions are clearly mediated by a well planned organization of the space, that favours not only interactions among children but also their interactions with adults. The spatial arrangements have to be continually reviewed according to the children's changing developmental abilities and interests. Organization of space in group settings that provides circumscribed areas for various activities and allows an easy visual or motor access to the caregiver favours the interaction among the children. It also helps to focus their attention, giving them opportunities to choose among various alternatives and to spend more profitable time in that activity. Thus, it provides more opportunities for interaction and learning for all children. Through low-cost adaptations of the environment, e.g. structuring the space with circumscribed zones, caregivers may promote interactions among children without their direct mediation. They might then become more available to establish contact with an individual child or with a subgroup, and thus contribute to the improvement of quality of care and education in group settings for young children. Circumscribed zones can also be created in outdoor spaces using all the available facilities that the outdoors provides. This can be achieved using various materials, different textures, constructing tunnels or huts, or digging little channels where water can flow. In such group settings, the same-age peers are the most available partners for interaction. The adult has an important supportive and structuring role, but other children strongly attract the child's interest, although he or she may look for the adult's proximity and help, particularly in stressful situations (Camaioni 1980; Rossetti-Ferreira *et al.* 1985).

Babies' interactions with peers

The emphasis on adult–child interaction in early childhood education and care has somehow hindered the opportunity to discuss the value of early peer interaction on child development. For a long period, children under three years of age have been considered to be unable to establish complex and lasting interactions with same-age peers, although interest in other children's behaviour has been widely recognized even in early infancy (Schaffer 1984). More recently, and as noted in Chapter 1 of this volume, early peer interaction research has been receiving more academic attention. This has coincided with the increase in group care and education arrangements for babies and toddlers in many different parts of the world (Rossetti-Ferreira *et al.* 2002).

Some possible challenges to be addressed when conducting observations of babies' interactions are the conditions of investigation and the understanding or definition of interaction itself. Most observational studies of babies have been carried out in home environments, where there are few children, and even fewer same-age peers. In those environments, the preferred partner is most often an adult, usually the mother. In contrast, in a daycare context, there are more children and the adult:child ratio is much lower. Consequently, the researcher has more possibilities to observe and to understand the interactive processes between children, even very young ones. In this quite recent context, the interactive process between babies is beginning to be investigated. However, it requires an adequate conceptualization of interaction, which enables researchers to capture and reveal the special features of interactions that occur during the first year of life.

According to Franchi e Vasconcelos *et al.* (2003), when babies' interactions are observed using the adult–child model, babies' interactions may not make sense, as they have quite different characteristics compared to older children's or adults' interactions. They appear more fragmented, do not have a clear script, may start as an unplanned encounter, or even initiated due to the babies' immature motor coordination, all of which can even favour exchanges between them. At that early age, often as a result of such motor immaturity, the interactive episodes may be short lived and disorganized. However, that awkwardness may actually prolong the interactive episode between young infants and/or even stimulate the emergence of new interactive episodes. Thus, although it was always recognized that young babies observe other children with great interest, the idea that there was in fact an interaction between them begins only to be considered when we observe in more detail how those interactions occur and develop. Examples of such interactions can be followed up at the two episodes presented in Figures 7.2 to 7.9 (Costa 2008).

One of the episodes shows two eleven-month-old babies. One of them (with the soother) picks up the toy the other is playing with (Figure 7.2). The other begins to cry (Figure 7.3) and, after a while, she goes after the former, trying to recover the lost object. To do that, within a silent dialogue, the baby girl uses diverse gestures to negotiate with her partner, either asking for the object (with the palm of the hand turned up) (Figure 7.4) or trying to pick it up (with the palm of the hand turned down) (Figure 7.5).

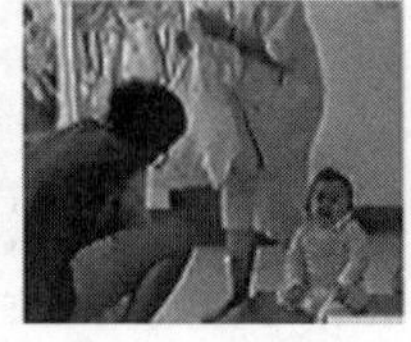

Figure 7.2–7.5
Source: Copyright Carolina Alexandre Costa

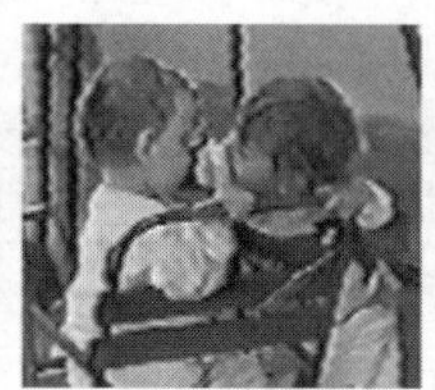
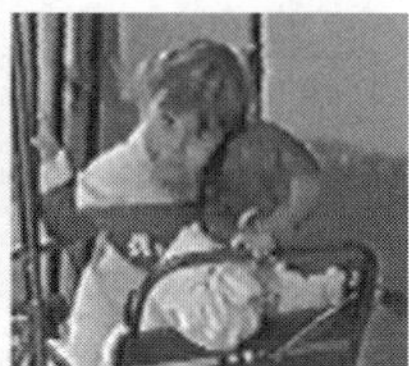

Figure 7.6–7.9
Source: Copyright Carolina Alexandre Costa

The second episode presents Reis (a 13-month-old boy) and Arthur (an 11-month-old), both playing at the childcare centre outdoor area. Arthur is in the swing and Reis approaches him, making a series of movements, expressions and gestures of interest and caresses toward the partner, both children smiling widely during interaction (Figures 7.6–7.9).

The study of Anjos *et al.* (2004), who based their investigation on a detailed analysis of episodes of babies during their first year of life, also revealed peer interaction at that early age. Through that analysis, interactions were shown to be frequent, although brief, fluid and easily interrupted. Moreover, analysis pointed out that the interaction goes far beyond *doing something together,* as Carvalho, Império-Hamburger and Pedrosa (1997) have already suggested. Children presented reciprocal and not necessarily intentional regulation, through which behaviours were guided and transformed only by focusing and having attention on the other child. Thus, even from a distance, their behaviours could be regulated while being involved in diverse activities, and even if one of them was not aware that he/she was regulating the other partner's behaviour.

Thus, based on these theoretical-methodological approaches, it was possible to consider and understand dialogue and meanings emerging among babies, although they were not structured by verbal means. Additionally, infants, at the end of their first year of life in childcare contexts, were observed to demonstrate both empathy and pretend play behaviours (Amorim *et al.* 2008).

In the first case, empathy was observed in a 13-month-old boy's behaviour directed towards a younger peer girl (a nine-month-old) who was crying when her caregiver disappeared behind the door, as can be seen in Figures 7.10 to 7.12.

 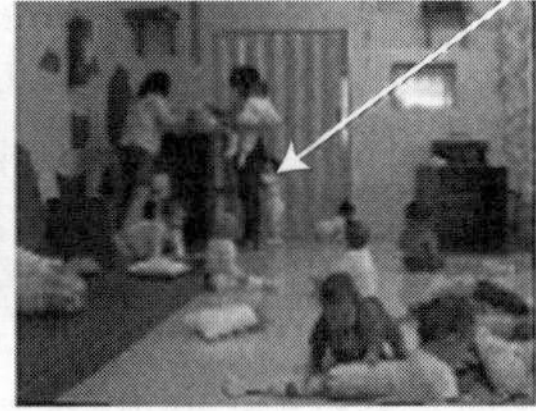 

Figure 7.10–7.12
Source: Copyright Adriana Mara dos Anjos

Figure 7.13–7.15
Source: Copyright Adriana Mara dos Anjos

As the baby girl was dramatically crying in front of the closed door, inside which was the caregiver, the older boy seemed to try to help her by opening the door (Figure 7.10). However, neither were able to open it. Then the boy can be seen trying to gain another caregiver's attention, by pulling her clothes (Figure 7.11). As no solution was reached, the boy pats the young girl's head, as if to comfort her (Figure 7.12).

In the other episode, the same 13-month-old boy can be seen paying a great deal of attention to an 11-month-old infant boy, who was passing by him (Figure 7.13).

Afterwards, he acts as if the younger one was going to pick the object up from him. Then, repeatedly and joyfully, he begins to run away from the younger boy, searching for a place far away from him (Figure 7.14) and also running into his mother's lap (Figure 7.15).

What is going on in young children's interactions?

To understand the possibility opened up by peer interactions to children's development we have carried out other investigations regarding the way young children interact with same-age partners. Using the concept of role as an interactional category, our focus was on the way peers coordinated the roles they perform in their interactions. This role playing was conceived as a dynamic process, within which occur alternate movements either of expansion or constriction, constrained by shared meanings that organize the partners' play and interactions.

Based on these conceptions, we analyzed semi-longitudinal data of peer interactions in two groups of 21- to 48-month-old children, who attended a Brazilian public childcare centre for low-income families for ten to twelve hours per day. Ten sessions, of nine minutes each, per group (group A = five children and group B = eight children) in children's playrooms were recorded during a twelve-month period. The space was sparsely resourced and its area, approximately 25 m^2, was equipped with some small mattresses, chairs and a small table. Some objects such as toys, plastic blocks and items of clothing were available in boxes or shelves. For each six-hour period, there was one caregiver taking charge of 18 children (Oliveira 1988; Oliveira and Rossetti-Ferreira 1996).

A microanalysis of the sessions allowed us to track the emergence of new forms of reacting to an interaction partner. This was through assuming a role as a way to attribute some meaning to the ongoing situation and by negotiating a shared meaning for a common, although brief, play episode. A fragmented and syncretic character of the children's representations in very short periods of gesture complementation around a script was revealed. See Figures 7.16 and 7.17.

> Episode 1 – Telma (23 months old) and Vania (21 months old) are seated side by side, playing with some wooden blocks. Vania, with a serious face, rubs carefully a block on another, as if rubbing a soap on a sponge, and then carefully she rubs one of the blocks from the front to the back of Telma's head, in a gesture similar to combing her hair, and with her face quite close to Telma's, she says: 'Pretty, isn't it?', smiling and moving her head affirmatively.

It is interesting to observe that these 21- to 23-month-old girls explored the situations mainly by expressive gestures and postural adjustments that reproduce quite well the postures, expressions and verbalizations that occur in their cultural environment. A wooden block and the partner's close presence are used by both children as props for their actions in a here-and-now frame. They enact some personally experienced scripts in the play situation, through highly imitative gestures. It is also possible to notice that the children seem to have some difficulty dissociating two interrelated

Figure 7.16–7.17
Source: Copyright Zilma M. Ramos Oliveira

scripts involved in the daily activity of washing the hair at home and at the childcare centre – gesture of rubbing a soap/sponge in the peer's hair – and combing the hair – gesture of rubbing a small wooden block from the front to the back of her peer's hair. This global interpretation of the situation and the difficulty of planning in advance a detailed and integrated script for a joint action transform their play into a kind of collage of fragments of well-known routines that are experienced daily either at their own homes or at the childcare centre.

The study of all sessions of the two groups revealed the highly complex situation being analyzed and it indicated some aspects in which the young children showed an improvement when coordinating the roles they play in the ongoing situation. At first, the children's gestures act as effective prompts for initiating the activities. Their emotional expression and postural adjustments create a kind of language that models their gestures while they interact. On the other hand, in this initial period, the children's imitations increasingly transform the original elements that are brought into the present situation by the partner's actions.

> Episode 2 – John (23 months old) approaches a big metal cylinder containing building blocks, which is being moved up and down rhythmically by Vivi (21 months old) and leans on it with one hand. Standing up and without moving away, John lowers and raises his trunk while flexing his knees, accompanying the rhythm with which Vivi moves the cylinder. He then takes his hand off the cylinder and moves his arms up and down in the same rhythm without swaying his body.

> Episode 3 – (5 months later) John and Vivi stand up side by side holding wooden hammers. They jump up and down with a joyful expression repeatedly shouting 'Hei!' (he after she) and hit the same wooden toy with their hammers.

Another way children coordinate their participation in the interactions they create is by using verbal expressions that focus the other's attention on an object, or point out an alternation of turns.

> Episode 4 – Telma (25 months old) holds out an object in the direction of Vivi (23 months old at that observation) saying: 'Look, Vivi!'

> Episode 5 – Fabio (45 months old) and Fernando (45 months old) are holding little wooden boxes. Fabio tells Fernando: 'Now me!', and starts hitting the lid of his box. When Fabio stops hitting, Fernando says: 'Now me!' and hits the lid of his box. Fabio then says 'Now me!' and hits the lid of his box. Fernando says 'Now me!' and does the same.

The emerging use of verbal language by the children to call the partner's attention in the episodes helped the children to coordinate their roles through joint attention and alternation of turns in episodes 3, 4 and 5. Coming back to episode 1, it is also possible to notice that in it the children begin to integrate their roles in their interactions through the use of verbal expressions that are part of well-known daily scripts 'Pretty, isn't it?' In this way, the children can verbally assign some elements that are culturally constitutive of the roles being constructed by their actions. As verbal language becomes more functional in mediating their role coordination, a better organization of common activities can be observed during children's interactions. Their better linguistic mastery allows older children not only to suggest activities to their peers or to organize the props and scenery, but also to check one's own role ('I'm the mother, right?'), to propose a theme for a common play ('I want to play mummy') or to assign the partner a role ('You are going to be the daughter'). These data provide a new perspective on young-peer interactions as a locus for knowledge construction and psychological development, a space for novelty and imagination (Oliveira and Valsiner 1997).

Challenges and implications for research

In order to tackle most of the issues regarding young children's care and education and to improve the quality of the children's developmental conditions in Brazil, a network of dynamically interrelated activities has been considered and developed by our research group. This includes research, training and education of human resources, consultation and guidance, production of written and audiovisual materials, and involvement in public policies, among others (Rossetti-Ferreira 1992).

In a research programme aimed at investigating in more detail the conditions that either favour or hinder babies' and young children's interactions, it is proposed that the exclusive focus on the dyad needs to be enlarged to include the surrounding socio-cultural context. This is necessary in order to investigate how children's interactions are mediated, promoted or broken up, and how emotions, relationships and meaning construction emerge in the context of group settings. This requires training in a new way of observing children's actions and interactions, which is informed by knowledge. When one looks at the scenes and episodes described in this chapter for the first time, an initial response may be to conclude that nothing is happening among the children. It is only when you revisit the scenes slowly, frame by frame, that you begin to make sense of what the children are doing and what one can see.

In summary, the psycho-pedagogical approach of childcare centres should be based on the conception of young children as able communicators, whose interactional competencies are constructed in structured environments in which the young children can interact and play with peers. That guideline must orient in-service training for educators. Pedagogical practices should support children's development of autonomy, responsibility, solidarity, respect for the common well-being and a democratic order. That is the way forward, we believe, for the construction of identities that are affirmative, persistent and able to assume cooperative actions in relation to knowledge and values.

Acknowledgement

We would like to acknowledge the financial support of FAPESP, CAPES and CNPq for the research reported in this chapter.

Point for reflection and discussion

Rossetti-Ferreira *et al.* argue that we need a new understanding or definition of interaction when studying peer interactions of babies in group settings. They give several examples of behaviour of babies that inspired them to rethink their conceptualization of interaction. What do they see that could not be seen or understood in earlier studies? Make a short video of young children interacting with each other and try to analyze their interactions frame by frame. Discuss the operationalization of 'interaction' that you (implicitly) use.

Note

1 The ideas and many of the studies presented in this chapter have been developed by the Brazilian Investigation Center on Human Development and Early Child Education (CINDEDI), which initiated its activities at the University of São Paulo in the late 1970s, became a formal institution in the 1990s, and was recognized by UNESCO in 1996 (UNESCO 1996). The various investigators of CINDEDI are involved in dynamically interrelated activities, such as research, training and education of human resources; consultation and guidance for daycare centers and foster institutions; production of teaching materials and didactic scientific videos, among others. They are often involved in political actions to press for policies to improve the developmental conditions of young children and adolescents in Brazil, helping its implementation, whenever possible (Rossetti-Ferreira 1992).

Bibliography

Amorim, K.S., Anjos, A.M. and Rossetti-Ferreira, M.C. (2008) 'Do babies interact with babies? Didactic/Scientific DVD', Ribeirão Preto: Pseudo Vídeo.

Anjos, A.M., Amorim, K.S. and Rossetti-Ferreira, M.C. (2004) 'Processos interativos de bebês em creche' [Babies interactive processes at daycare]. *Estudos de Psicologia (Natal)*, 9: 513–22.

Bomfim, J. and Campos-de-Carvalho, M.I. (2002) 'Arranjos espaciais e ocupação do espaço por crianças de 1–2 e 3–4 anos em creches' [Spatial arrangements and occupation of 1–2 and 3–4 years old children at day care]. In Pós-Graduação em Psicologia e Educação da Faculdade de Filosofia, Ciências e Letras de Ribeirão Preto (Org). *Livro de Artigos do V Seminário de Pesquisa* [*Annals of the 5th Psychological Research Seminar*], 139–48.

Bomfim, J. and Campos-de-Carvalho, M. (2006) 'Intercambios sociales en niños de 1–2 años y arreglos espaciales en guarderías brasileñas' [*Social exchanges in 1–2 years old children and spatial arrangements in Brazilians daycare centres*]. *Medio Ambiente y Comportamiento Humano* (*Environment and Human Behaviour*), 7: 67–88.

Brasil (1988) Congresso Nacional. *Constituição da República Federativa do Brasil (Brazilian Constitution)*. Brasília, DF.

Camaioni, L. (1980) *L'Interazione Tra Bambini [Babies' Interactions]*. Roma: Editora Armando.

Campos-de-Carvalho, M.I. (2004) 'Use of space by children in day care centers'. *Revista de Etologia* [*Ethological Journal*], 6: 41–8.

Campos-de-Carvalho, M.I. and Mingorance, R.C. (1999) 'Zonas circunscritas e ocupação do espaço por crianças pequenas em creche' [*Circumscribed zones and space occupation by young children at day care*]. *Revista InterAmericana de Psicologia* [*Journal of InterAmerican Psychology*], 33: 67–89.

Campos-de-Carvalho, M.I. and Rossetti-Ferreira, M.C. (1993) 'Importance of spatial arrangements for young children in day care centers'. *Children's Environments,* 10: 19–30.

Carvalho, A.M.A., Império-Hamburger, A. and Pedrosa, M.I. (1997) 'Interaction, regulation and correlation: a conceptual discussion and empirical examples in the context of human development'. In M. Lyra and J. Valsiner (eds) *The Construction of Psychological Processes in the Course of Interpersonal Communication.* Norwood: Ablex.

Costa, C.A. (2008) 'Processo de 'abreviação' em relações de bebês com seus pares de idade' *['Abbreviation' process in babies' relationships with their peers].* Monografia de Bacharelado [*Undergraduate monograph*] em Psicologia do Depto. de Psicologia e Educação da Faculdade de Filosofia, Ciências e Letras de Ribeirão Preto da Universidade de São Paulo.

Franchi e Vasconcelos, C.R., Amorim, K.S., Anjos, A.M. and Rossetti-Ferreira, M.C. (2003) 'A incompletude como virtude: interação de bebês na creche' [Incompleteness as a virtue: a daycare center babies' interaction]. *Psicologia Reflexão e Crítica,* 16: 293–301.

Hartup, W.W. (1996) 'The company they keep: friendships and their developmental significance'. *Child Development*, 67: 1–13.

Kulhman Jr., M. (1991) 'Instituições pré-escolares assistencialistas no Brasil' [Philantropic pre-school institutions in Brazil]. *Cadernos de Pesquisa* [*Research Journal*], 78: 17–26.

Legendre, A. (1989) 'Young children's social competences and their use of space in day-care centers'. In B.H. Schneider, G. Attili, J. Nadel and R. Weissberg (eds) *Social Competence in Developmental Perspective.* Holland: Kluwer.

Lyra, M.C. and Rossetti-Ferreira, M.C. (1995) 'Transformation and construction in social interaction: a new perspective of analysis of mother-infant dyad'. In J. Valsiner (ed) *Child Development within Culturally Structured Environments III.* Norwood, N.J.: Ablex Publishing Corp.

Olds, A.R. (1987) 'Designing settings for infants and toddlers'. In C.S. Weinstein and T.G. David (eds) *Spaces for Children – The Built Environment and Child Development.* New York: Plenum.

Oliveira, Z.M.R. (1988) 'Jogos de papéis: uma perspectiva para análise do desenvolvimento humano' [*Role play: a perspective for the analysis of human development*]. Unpublished thesis. São Paulo: Universidade de São Paulo.

Oliveira, Z.M.R. and Rossetti-Ferreira, M.C. (1996) 'Understanding the co-constructive nature of human development: role coordination in early peer interaction'. In J. Valsiner and H.-G. Voss (eds) *The Structure of Learning Processes.* Norwood, N.J.: Ablex Publishing Corp.

Oliveira, Z.M.R. and Valsiner, J. (1997) 'Play and Imagination: the psychological construction of novelty'. In A. Fogel, M.C.P. Lyra and J. Valsiner (eds) *Dynamics and Indeterminism in Developmental and Social Processes.* Mahwah, N.J., Lawrence Earbaum.

Proshansky, H.M., Ittelson, W.H. and Rivlin, L. (eds) (1970) *Environmental Psychology: Man and his Physical Settings.* New York: Holt, Rinehart & Winston.

Rossetti-Ferreira, M.C. (1988) 'A pesquisa na universidade e a educação da criança pequena' [*The research at the university and early child education*]. *Cadernos de Pesquisa* [*Research Journal*], 67: 59–63.

——(1992) 'Current activities of the Brazilian research center on early child development and education'. *ISSDB Newsletter,* 2: 3–4.

Rossetti-Ferreira, M.C., Ramon, F. and Barreto, A.R. (2002) 'Improving early child care and education in developing countries'. In C. von Hofsten and L. Bäckman (eds) *Social, Developmental and Clinical Perspectives: Vol. 2.* England: Psychology Press.

Rossetti-Ferreira, M.C., Secaf-Silveira, R.E., Blurton-Jones, N.G., Farquhar-Brown and MacDonald-Moore, L. (1985) 'Adult–child and peer interaction during brief separations'. *British Journal of Developmental Psychology,* 3: 163–73.

Schaffer, H.R. (1984) *The Child's Entry into a Social World.* London: Academic Press.

Secaf-Silveira, R.E., Picolo, T., Delphino, V.R.P, Faria, L.M. and Rossetti-Ferreira, M.C. (1987) 'Oportunidades de contacto entre o adulto e a criança em creche' [*Opportunities for contact between the adult and the child at day care*]. *Revista Brasileira de Estudos Pedagógicos* [*Brazilian Journal of Pedagogical Studies*], 158: 130–63.

UNESCO (1996) *Early Childhood Care & Education, Directory of Organizations in Latin America and The Caribbean*. UNESCO, p. 83, BR043.

Vygotsky, L.S. (1978) *Mind in Society*. Cambridge, M.A.: Harvard University Press.

——(1986) *Thought and Language, 2nd edition*. Cambridge, M.A.: MIT Press.

Wallon, H. (1942) *De l'acte a la pensée: essai de psychologie comparée [From Act to Thought]*. Paris: Flammarion.

Chapter 8

Fostering a sense of belonging in multicultural childcare settings

Elly Singer and Dorian de Haan[1]

Parents, peers, teachers and the group

When babies or toddlers enter into group childcare facilities, they begin to participate in a social life outside the family. They develop friendships with peers and a sense of belonging to their group. They have conflicts and learn peacemaking strategies (Singer and de Haan 2007). Young children are much more like adults than we thought before. They can react just as strongly to injustice as adults, but their approach is different. They are inclined to slap their opponent instead of using words. If they have hurt someone, the feeling of guilt is often clearly visible on their faces. In fact, young children can do some things better than adults. They are much more forgiving; their quarrels are over much more quickly (Rourou *et al.* 2006). Even so, we should not overestimate young children. They need their parents and trusted teachers as a secure base from which they can go out into the world. Teachers have to ensure that children feel safe and confident among themselves. A good childcare centre is characterized by positive relations among the children and a happy 'we-feeling' in the group (Figure 8.1).

Multicultural settings

The social life of young children in the group is related in many ways to the surrounding cultural communities. Teachers bring in their experiences of their own upbringing, professional training and belief systems from the particular communities in which they participate. According to Harkness and Super (1999) and Huijbregts *et al.* (2008) the personal beliefs of teachers stem from two sources: everyday personal experience with colleagues and childrearing in the childcare centre, and socially shared cultural beliefs on childrearing within the particular community to which they belong. Children also bring their home experiences with their parents and siblings, and elements of the cultural community of their family.

Nowadays, childcare centres in Western countries face increasing cultural diversity among the teachers and the children and parents. Teachers, young children and their parents from Western and non-Western countries are working and living together within the same childcare system. In a multicultural society, teachers, parents and children are confronted with several cultural belief systems on child rearing that may

Figure 8.1 Tummy tickle.
Source: Copyright Project Singer 2007

differ in numerous ways (Kağitçibaşi 2005). However, the current philosophies and methods of early childhood education, research and childrearing are mainly developed in Western countries and based on individualistic child-centred models (Singer 1993; Rosenthal 1999).

To capture the differences between Western and non-Western cultures the individualism–collectivism distinction is often used. This distinction refers to belief systems stressing individuality, competition and independent selfhood versus relatedness, cooperation and interdependent selfhood. Individualism and collectivism should not be conceived as dichotomous, but as graded, interrelated and multidimensional. Individualistic and collectivistic beliefs are found to coexist in most cultures, depending on social contexts and specific social situations. But nevertheless there are differences in Western and non-Western cultures in the emphasis they lay on individualistic or collectivistic beliefs and values.

In the Netherlands there have been several studies of relationships in multicultural childcare centres that are based on the individualism–collectivism dimension. In this chapter we will discuss what these studies have revealed about peer relations of young children in the context of multicultural childcare settings. Do children develop a sense of togetherness along ethnic lines? And what do teachers and parents do to support positive relationships among children of different cultural backgrounds?

Early child education and care in the Netherlands

Before we discuss the studies in multicultural settings, we will give a short outline of the Dutch context and early childhood education and care system. In the Netherlands about 11 per cent of the 17 million inhabitants, are first- or second-generation migrants from non-Western countries (Nederlandse Gezinsraad 2005). Most of these migrants come originally from the former Dutch colonies of Suriname (South America) and the Antilles (the Caribbean) and from Morocco and Turkey as descendents of the guest workers who were recruited to work in Dutch industry in the 1960s and 1970s. Additionally there are smaller groups of refugees from Asia, Africa and South America as well as foreign workers from inside and outside Europe.

In the Netherlands 25 per cent of children under four years old are enrolled in daycare facilities for working parents (Centraal Bureau Statistiek 2009). The dominant group in childcare centres is children from native Dutch families with higher educated parents who work outside the home. Most Dutch mothers work part time, while fathers work full time. Migrant mothers are increasingly working outside the home, but their participation in the labour market differs from ethnic group to group. Migrant children, especially those whose families are originally from Turkey and Morocco, often participate in educational playgroups and pre-schools. The programmes of these playgroups and pre-schools aim to prepare young children from disadvantaged families – because of home language or educational level of the parents – for entrance to the formal school system. Finally there are play groups for children of mothers who do not participate in the labour force to socialize with peers and to get acquainted with group life. Most children in the Netherlands (95 per cent) participate in the formal education system (primary school) from the age of four years.

Centres for childcare and education fall under the responsibility of the Ministry of Education or the department of education of the local municipality. Centres have to be licensed and are regularly supervised for quality. In general the group size for babies is nine babies with two teachers; and the toddlers (two- and three-year-olds) are in groups of fourteen children with two teachers. The research that we will discuss are studies of toddler groups in multicultural daycare centres and educational playgroups in urban areas.

Cultural differences in peer conflicts and friendships

Cross-cultural studies of peer conflicts provide a good window into diversity among young children, for instance, with regard to different conflict resolution strategies prevalent in different cultural groups. For example, the strategy of 'discussion', i.e. highly stylized and dramatic public discussions, used by pre-schoolers in Italy was not found in North-American children (Corsaro 2004). German pre-schoolers used a more distant type of contact to negotiate, such as smiling and talking, while Italian pre-schoolers used more bodily contact (Hold-Cavell *et al.* 1986). In some cultures the parents or teachers teach children rhymes and songs as means of reconciliation

Figure 8.2 Adapting to younger children.
Source: Copyright Project Singer 2007

after a conflict (Butovskaya *et al.* 2000). In some studies cultural differences in peer conflicts are related to the individualism–collectivism dimension. Sanchez Medina *et al.* (2001) found differences in why children have conflicts. Children from Andalusia, a more collectivistic culture, entered more often into conflict to carry out social actions; while children from the Netherlands, a more individualistic culture, tended to enter into conflict to negotiate their private space. Studies of older children show that individuals in collectivistic cultures tended to prefer procedures that reduce animosity between opponents belonging to the same group. They do not want to destroy long-term interpersonal relationships and try to refrain from open disputes. In the case of conflict with a non-group member, bystanders will support the member of their own group because of group loyalty (Bierbrauer and Klinger 2005; Markus and Kitayama 1991). Conversely, individuals from individualistic cultures are more likely to employ direct confrontations and independent conflict styles. They seem to be less worried about the potential harm of interpersonal relationships and more focused on securing their rights or in finding 'the truth' (Figure 8.2).

Peer conflicts in Dutch multicultural centres

What was found in the Dutch multicultural centres? In general, we did not find differences between the cultural groups (Rourou *et al.* 2006). In a study of two- and three-year-old children from native Dutch, Moroccan and Antillean backgrounds we found that the children have conflicts that relate to living in a group with same age mates. Conflicts provided opportunities to co-construct social rules and to get to know the opinions of others. The kind of rules that children co-construct became clear when we looked at the content of their conflicts. Most conflicts we found had to do with unwelcome physical contact. The children had to learn that there is a boundary between wrestling or romping around and really hurting each other. On the one hand physical contact was the way young children who function primarily at a non-verbal level make contact. But on the other hand they must learn to keep away and leave the other child alone if he or she wants to be left in peace and quiet. We discovered that the children had to cope with two rules: 'don't hurt each other' and 'don't disturb each other'. Conflicts about objects were also very frequent. The children had to learn to negotiate about two apparently opposing rules. Teachers said that they have to share toys or to take turns; and for joint play sharing toys is often a necessity. But teachers also referred to 'respect for personal ownership', and instructed children not to touch objects of another child. Then there were the 'I-want-to-join-in' conflicts with again two opposing rules: the rule that all children are welcome and allowed to join in; and the rule that children who play together do not want to be disturbed by a newcomer. Lastly there were conflicts about play ideas. For instance two children want to pretend play 'mother and baby', but neither of them want to play the baby role. In these conflicts children may learn the rules of negotiation (Figure 8.3).

Conflicts about unwelcome physical contact and objects were the most frequent among younger children, the two-year-olds in our study. Conflicts about play ideas were the most frequent among the three-year-olds. And 'I-want-to-join-in' conflicts were the most frequent in conflicts between younger and older children. The younger ones rejected the older ones just as often as the older children rejected the younger. With regard to frequency of conflict, seriousness, duration and reasons of conflict we did not find significant differences between the three cultural groups. We found only one significant difference: the duration of the conflicts of the Dutch children was longer compared with the Moroccan children. Maybe this longer perseverance of the Dutch children may be related to a more individualistic orientation in their upbringing. We did not find differences in the conflict resolution strategies that the children used. The Moroccan, Antillean and native Dutch children did not differ with regard to hitting, pushing or other forms of physical enforcing behaviour. Children of the three groups also used about the same amount of explorative, problem-solving actions or submissive actions (Singer and de Haan 2007). We did, however, find a significant cultural difference in peer interventions in peer conflicts by a child nearby. When children were bystanders in a peer conflict, all children tended to look to the teacher for help. But when there was no teacher available, Moroccan and Antillean children tended to intervene more often in the peer conflict than native Dutch children. One possible explanation accounting for this is that maybe the Moroccan and Antillean children are more inclined to feel responsible for peers than the Dutch children; this might reflect the more collectivistic values in their upbringing at home (Hoogdalem *et al.* 2008).

Figure 8.3 Learning the skills of negotiation.
Source: Copyright Project Singer 2007

Peer friendships in Dutch multicultural settings

Research by Howes and colleagues (Howes 1988, 1996; Howes and Ritchie 2002) and Vaughn and Santos (2009) shows that young children make friends from a very early age. Even one-year-olds often have a favourite playmate in childcare centres. These centre-based friendships can last for more than one year (Howes 1988). Anecdotal accounts of university students about lifelong friendships that started in childcare are not rare. According to a student of our research group, his friends made his childcare group safe, predictable, joyful and adventurous: 'As soon as I entered into the group, we looked for each other and played till the end of the day' (personal communication). In our Dutch studies on peer relations and friendship we observed eight childcare groups, each over a period of three or four months (Hoogdalem *et al.* submitted). Children who often played together also showed more mutual imitation and initiatives, and prosocial behaviour towards each other. The children showed their affinity by smiling, gently touching and helping behaviour. But they also showed their affinity by means of language (de Haan and Singer 2001). For instance they openly name friendship (Figure 8.4):

CAS (3 YEARS 5 MONTHS): 'You're my friend, aren't you?'
CHANTAL (TWO YEARS ELEVEN MONTHS): 'Yes'
CAS: 'And Bob's my friend too.'
CHANTAL: 'I am too, I am too, I'm Leanne's friend too'.

They expressed the desire to belong with each other by using nicknames. For instance, Sabine is called 'Silly-billy' and Emma 'Em' or 'Emmie'. And they create togetherness by imitation play with words:

KASPER: 'This puppy.'
CAS: 'You you you're this puppy.'
KASPER: 'You this poppy.'
CAS: 'No, you're this puppy. You're this puppy, this pup.'
KASPER: 'This pup.'
CAS: 'You are this pup, this, you're this pup.'
KASPER: 'You are this pup.'
CAS: 'And you're this poop!'

Typically, children affiliate with peers who are similar to them on key characteristics. Following Cranley Gallagher *et al.* (2007: 32) who found 'that children's peer groups form around shared values, behaviours, and beliefs', we hypothesized in our Dutch study that the same ethnicity would predict friendship in children. Friendship was defined as mutual preference and proximity, prosocial behaviour towards each other, initiatives, imitation and mutual positive affect. But we had to reject that hypothesis. The likelihood of becoming friends was not related to the ethnic backgrounds of the children (Hoogdalem *et al.* submitted). Children of the same sex had significantly more chance of becoming friends; and the smaller the age differences of the children, the greater the chance of becoming friends. We found some indications that the shared affinity with certain play activities may play a role. Boy–Boy dyads, for instance, often played with cars together; we did not find one single girl–girl dyad that played with cars. Girl–girl dyads more often played in the home corner. Finally we found that the time that children spend together in the group is also important for friendships. Probably young children need time for recurrent interactions to build up

Figure 8.4 Are you my friend?
Source: Copyright Project Singer 2007

expectations, such as shared scripts, rituals and patterns of non-verbal behaviour. In this respect Dutch childcare centres are not supportive of peer friendships. Most Dutch children go part time to childcare centres (one, two or three days per week) because their parents, mostly the mothers, work part time and the grandparents take care of their children at home. A group meant for 14 young children may be used by 34 different children during the week. So each day the children meet different children in the group than the day before. In our Dutch study we found that 44 per cent of the children had no friend. That is a higher percentage than the 25 per cent that was found in a study of young children by Howes (1996) and by Lindsey (2002). Maybe this finding is related to the low stability in the peer group in Dutch childcare centres. The continuity of peer group membership was also low. After five months we returned to the same groups to discover that only 28 per cent of peer dyads we had observed were still in the same group. So the opportunity for young children to keep friends is highly dependent on the decisions of their parents and teachers about their placement in childcare facilities and groups.

Cultural differences in teacher and parent belief systems and behaviour

Native Dutch and migrant parents often appreciate childcare and education for young children in group settings because of the possibility of peer contact and social learning (Dijke *et al.* 1994). Young children like to play with peers, and group settings offer ample opportunities in this regard. In practice, however, most centres do not have a pedagogical policy to foster peer relationships. The days that the children come to the centre are primarily determined by the working days of their part-time working mother and the availability of childcare places. Teachers and parents seldom take into account the friendship relations of the children. In general, Dutch teachers take care to have warm and personal contact with every individual child; and they structure the time and space, and use rituals to guide the children at the level of the whole group. But in the Netherlands teachers are not very focused on supporting friendships or positive relations in small subgroups (Kruif *et al.* 2009). In our studies we found, for instance, that during lunch time teachers seldom enter into group conversations in which more than one child is involved. They talk with one child at a time, mostly by giving directives on eating or behaviour, or by asking about a child's need for food or drink. The same pattern is found when teachers intervene in peer conflicts (Singer and de Haan 2007). Only in 16 per cent of the conflict interventions did the teachers try to support the good relationship of the two opponents. In most interventions the teachers address themselves to one of the opponents with directives or suggestions for good behaviour: 'Don't do that Tamar!'; 'What is our rule Jan? Every child gets a turn!'

In Dutch childcare centres during free play teachers do not often play with the children or enter into mutual interactions and conversations. Again the teachers are mostly involved in regulating the children's behaviour by friendly directives, comments and offering toys. They take on the role of 'stage manager' to facilitate free play (Jones and Reynolds 1992). From the perspective of the individual child, for only six per cent of the time during free play is she/he involved in high-level interactions with the teacher (Hoogdalem *et al.* submitted).

Huijbregts *et al.* (2008) studied cultural diversity in childrearing beliefs of teachers in Dutch childcare centres. The teachers came from native Dutch, Antillean, Turkish and Moroccan backgrounds. They found that the teachers differed in the individualism–collectivism dimension when they were asked about their general ideas about childrearing. The native Dutch teachers more often agreed with statements such as: 'Children should be allowed to disagree with their caregiver if they feel their own ideas are better'. While the migrant teachers more often agreed with statements such as: 'Children should follow rules to learn manners'. The differences between native Dutch and migrant teachers almost disappeared with regard to ideas about professional work with children in the context of childcare centres. Harkness and Super (1999) suggest that as teachers share the responsibility for a group of children together with one or two colleagues, they continuously need to attune to and discuss the childrearing approach of each other. In this way they develop a shared frame of reference. More collectivistic childrearing beliefs were only visible when the migrant teachers were the dominant group in the team (Huijbregts *et al.* 2008).

Cultural differences in mothers of young children

Cultural differences seem to depend on the issues at stake and situations that are discussed. In many situations native Dutch and migrant mothers share the same basic values and educational goals for young children. Besides that, there are also big differences in diverse migrant groups and within cultural groups. In a study of mothers from native Dutch, Antillean and Moroccan backgrounds about adult interventions in peer conflicts of young children the cultural differences varied according to the sort of conflict (Rourou *et al.* 2006). All mothers agreed that aggressive behaviour in peer conflicts is not acceptable; but Antillean mothers were more authoritarian in their intervention strategy than the native Dutch or Moroccan mothers. In a conflict about sharing toys, the native Dutch mothers differed from the Antillean and Moroccan mothers: they were much less oriented on learning to share. The native Dutch mothers are more often focused on learning to endure the frustration of 'not getting the object' and to respect individual rights of property.

Although these mothers had much in common, they tended to stress the differences when they were asked to evaluate the upbringing of children in other cultural groups. Almost all mothers engaged in negative stereotyping. Native Dutch mothers felt that migrant parents do not exercise adequate control; they speculate that migrant mothers physically punish their children; are too strict; discriminate against girls and women; and don't talk with their children. Some Dutch mothers also expressed their fear of aggressive behaviour of migrant male juveniles. According to the Antillean mothers, Dutch children get too much freedom; there is a lack of parental control, and lack of respect for their elders. 'Dutch children are even allowed to hit and scold their own mother!' They criticized the Dutch family because of a lack of warmth and too much individualism. Contrary to the Antillean mothers, several Moroccan mothers thought that the Dutch upbringing of young children is too strict and with too many rules. They point to the importance of indulging young children. 'They have to feel that they can totally depend on their mother, so, when you are older, you can depend on them'. According to these mothers, fostering dependence in children is important to foster strong family ties and reciprocal responsibilities.

But most of the mothers also tended to put their opinions into perspective. They stressed that they don't have much experience with members of another cultural group, and that they based their opinion on the media and incidental experiences in the school, childcare centre or in shops. Almost all mothers felt that they basically adhere to the values of their parents. But most mothers, and not only the migrant mothers, also spoke of adapting to changed circumstances. Many mothers compared their own upbringing in rural areas with their children's upbringing in urban areas. In their own youth they had much more freedom to play safely outside the home. Nowadays the parents have to be stricter and supervise more closely because there is less space for children, and parents and children spend more hours together inside the home. Family and neighbours are also less available to supervise children outside the home (Singer 2005).

The study of the mothers makes it clear that culture is dynamic and that they adapt their beliefs and behaviour under the influence of new experiences and contact with other groups. Most adaptations are related to issues of parental authority and discipline. In this respect there were no big differences between the ethnic groups. But the direction of the change in parenting style is different in the three groups. Most of the Antillean mothers said that they are as strict as their own parents. Most of the Dutch mothers said that they are less strict and that they give their children more freedom with certain boundaries. Most of the Moroccan mothers told about the change from a very permissive caring and indulgent attitude towards young children towards a more consistent and strict pedagogical attitude. The mothers of all three cultural groups welcomed the change to more openness in the parent–child relationship and more discussion.

In conclusion

The studies in Dutch multicultural childcare centres show that these centres can offer very good opportunities for young children from different cultural background to learn to play together and to solve their conflicts in constructive ways. We found few differences in friendship or conflicts in the children under four years old along ethnic and cultural lines. But the studies also show that the children may receive cultural messages from their parents and teachers in a way that might make children feel culturally inferior or superior as they grow older.

In general the native Dutch individualistic orientation dominates in the childcare centres. The individual rights and needs of the child and the family surpass the interest in fostering positive social relationships in children. The working hours of the parents are more important than the children's interest in stable groups and friendships. Dutch teachers are not very focused on fostering the relationships between individual children. They are more focused on personal contact with individual children and in managing the whole group. In educational programmes for migrant children they are focused on language development and parent education. However, we have to keep in mind that childcare in group settings is a relatively new phenomenon in the Netherlands. Recently much more attention is being paid to recognizing the educational value of the social lives of young children in childcare settings (Singer and de Haan 2007; Singer and Kleerekoper 2009).

All parents share the challenge to (re)invent tools to socialize their young children in current Western urban circumstances. Related to their cultural background they develop more openness towards children (the Antillean), more openness and less permissiveness (the Moroccan) and more openness within firm boundaries (the Dutch). We think that shared experiences in multicultural childcare centres and the acknowledgement of shared pedagogical challenges related to current life conditions can contribute to mutual understanding between parents and between practitioners of young children from different cultural backgrounds. Childcare centres can play an important role in community building in multicultural societies.

Point for reflection and discussion

In this chapter Singer and de Haan describe how the social lives of young children in multicultural settings are influenced dynamically by the surrounding cultural communities, including the views and priorities of parents, teachers and children. Consider an early years setting you are familiar with. To what extent do teachers reflect on, articulate and share their personal beliefs and values about childrearing? What happens when there are disagreements between staff and between staff and parents?

Note

1 Elly Singer is associate professor at the University of Utrecht and University of Amsterdam. Dorian de Haan is associate professor at the University of Utrecht and INHOLLAND University. They were involved in a wide range of studies of young children in group settings in the Netherlands focusing on gender and multicultural issues; joint play, humour and conflicts; (non) verbal communication and language development; teachers' roles and communication the children. Elly Singer is specialized in the history of early childhood education and care and in social emotional development. Dorian de Haan is specialized in language development and language education. Both participate in projects to improve the pedagogical quality of Dutch childcare centres.

Bibliography

Ahnert, L., Pinquart, M. and Lamb, M.E. (2006) 'Security of children's relationships with non-parental care providers: a meta-analysis'. *Child Development,* 74: 664–79.

Bierbrauer, G. and Klinger, E.W. (2005) 'The influence of conflict context characteristics on conflict regulation preferences of immigrants'. *Journal of Cross-Cultural Psychology,* 36: 340–54.

Butovskaya, M., Verbeek, P., Ljungberg, T. and Lunardini, A. (2000) 'A multicultural view of peacemaking among young children'. In F. Aureli and F.B.M. de Waal (eds) *Natural Conflict Resolution*. Berkeley: University of California Press.

Centraal Bureau Statistiek (2009) *Kinderopvang, 2007* [*Statistics daycare facilities, 2007*] www.cbs.nl/nl-NL/menu/themas/inkomen-bestedingen/cijfers/incidenteel/maatwerk/2008-wm-2452.htm (accessed 10 March 2010).

Corsaro, W. (2004) *The Sociology of Childhood,* 2nd edition. Thousand Oaks, C.A.: Pine Forge Press.

de Haan, D. and Singer, E. (2001) 'Young children's language of togetherness'. *International Journal of Early Years Education,* 9: 117–24.

Dijke, A. van, Terpstra, L. and Hermanns, J. (1994) *Ouders over kinderopvang [Parents's Opinions about Child Care]*. Amsterdam: SCO/Kohnstamm Instituut.

Gallagher, K.C., Dadisman, K., Farmer, T.W., Huss, L. and Hutchins, B.C. (2007) 'Social dynamics of early childhood classrooms'. In O.N. Saracho and B. Spodek (eds) *Contemporary Perspectives on Social Learning in Early Childhood Education*. Charlotte, N.C.: Information Age Publishing Inc.

Harkness, S. and Super, Ch. M. (1999) 'From parents' cultural belief systems to behaviour'. In L. Eldering and P.P.M. Leseman (eds) *Effective Early Education: Cross-Cultural Perspectives*. New York: Falmer Press, pp.67–90.

Hold-Cavell, B.C.L., Attili, G. and Aschleidt, M. (1986) 'A cross-cultural comparison of children's behaviour during their first year in a preschool'. *International Journal of Behavioural Development,* 9: 471–83.

Hoogdalem, A., Singer, E., Streck, L. and Bekkema, N. (2008) 'Young children who intervene in peer conflicts in multicultural child care centers'. *Behaviour,* 145: 1653–70.

Hoogdalem, A., Singer, E., Eek, A. and Heesbeen, D. (submitted) 'Friends or just playmates? A study of the relationship characteristics in peer groups of young children in Dutch day care centers'.

Howes, C. (1988) 'Peer interaction of young children'. *Monographs of the Society for Research in Child Development,* 53: 1–92.

——(1996). 'The earliest friendships'. In W.M. Bukowski, A.F. Newcomb and W.W. Hartup (eds) *The Company they Keep*. New York: Cambridge University Press.

Howes, C. and Ritchie, S. (2002) *A Matter of Trust: Connecting Teachers and Learners in the Early Childhood Classroom*. New York/London: Teachers College Press.

Huijbregts, S.K., Leseman, P.P.M. and Tavecchio, L.W. (2008) 'Cultural diversity in center-based childcare: childrearing beliefs of professional caregivers from different cultural communities in the Netherlands'. *Early Childhood Research Quarterly,* 23: 233–45.

Jones, E. and Reynolds, G. (1992) *The Play's the Thing: Teachers' Roles in Children's Play*. New York: Teachers College Press.

Kağitçibaşi, C. (2005) 'Autonomy and relatedness in cultural context. Implications for self and family'. *Journal of Cross-Cultural Psychology,* 36: 403–22.

Kontos, S. (1999) 'Preschool teacher's talk, roles, and activity settings during free play'. *Early Childhood Research Quarterly,* 14: 363–82.

Kruif, R.E.L., Riksen-Walraven, J.M.A., Gevers Deynoot-Schaub, M.J.J.M. *et al.* (2009) *Pedagogische kwaliteit van de opvang van 0–4-jarigen in Nederlandse kinderdagverblijven in 2008 [Pedagogical quality of Dutch childcare centres for 0–4 year olds]*. Amsterdam: NCKO.

Lindsey, E.W. (2002) 'Preschool children's friendships and peer acceptance: links to social competence'. *Child Study Journal*, 32: 145–56.

Markus, H.R. and Kitayama, S. (1991) 'Culture and the self: implications for cognition, emotion, and motivation'. *Psychological Review,* 98: 224–53.

Nederlandse Gezinsraad (2005) *Signalement 3/A Allochtone gezinnen: Feiten en cijfers*. [Migrant families: facts and numbers]. The Hague: Nederlandse Gezinsraad.

Rosenthal, M.K. (1999) 'Out-of-home childcare research: a cultural perspective'. *International Journal of Behavioral Development,* 23: 477–518.

Rourou, A., Singer, E., Bekkema, N. and de Haan, D. (2006) 'Cultural perspectives on peer conflicts in multicultural Dutch child care centres'. *European Early Childhood Education and Research Association Journal,* 14: 35–55.

Sanchez Medina, J.A., Martinez Lozano, V. and Goudena, P.P. (2001) 'Conflict management in preschoolers: a cross-cultural perspective'. *International Journal of Early Years Education,* 9: 153–60.

Singer, E. (1993) 'Shared care for children'. *Theory & Psychology,* 3: 429–49.

——(2005) 'The liberation of the child: a recurrent theme in the history of education in western societies'. *Early Childhood Development and Care,* 175: 611–20.

Singer, E. and de Haan, D. (2007) 'Social life of young children. Co-construction of shared meanings and togetherness, humor, and conflicts in child care centers'. In B. Spodek and O.N. Saracho (eds) *Contemporary Perspectives on Research in Early Childhood Social Learning*. Charlotte, N.C.: Information Age Publishers.

Singer, E. and Kleerekoper, L. (2009) *Pedagogisch kader kindercentra 0–4 jaar* [*National curriculum and pedagogical framework for child care centres for 0–4 year olds*] Maarssen: Elsevier gezondheid.

Vaughn, B.E. and Santos, A.J. (2009) 'Structural descriptions of social interactions among young children. Affiliation and dominance in preschool groups'. In K.H. Rubin, W.M. Bukowski and B.P. Laursen (eds) *Handbook of Peer Interactions, Relationships, and Groups*. New York: Guilford Press.

Chapter 9

Including children with disabilities

Promoting peer relationships and friendships

Nina von der Assen and Margaret Kernan[1]

Introduction

Children with disabilities have the same rights as their non-disabled peers, and should have equal opportunities to play experiences and opportunities to develop friendships in early years settings. Many early childhood education and care settings have adopted an inclusive approach, i.e. including children with disabilities in their programmes.

In a number of countries benefits of inclusive settings to all children are increasingly recognized, particularly with regard to their potential in enhancing children's apprecia-tion of diversity, their acceptance and valuing of individual differences, and learning to help and support each other. This is an ethical and pedagogical issue.

The nature of young children's peer relations and status in peer groups may influence adjustments in later years (Wolfberg *et al.* 1999). Research suggests that attitudes towards children with disabilities become increasingly negative in primary school (Dyson 2005). Thus, the early years mark a critical point at which children's attitudes to those who are perceived as 'different' begin to emerge.

Our intention in this chapter is to explore the role of peer relationships in the active participation of young children with disabilities in organized early childhood education and care settings. First, we will give an overview of children with disabilities and early childhood education within a human rights framework. Then, we will look at research in the field of inclusion of children with disabilities and friendship in early childhood education and care settings. Finally, we will discuss the implications of this research for practice. It should be noted that the majority of the studies cited were undertaken in the United States, Canada and the United Kingdom.

Rights of young children with disabilities to participate in early childhood education and care

The United Nations Convention on the Rights of the Child (UNCRC) (United Nations 1989) applies to all children irrespective of colour, sex, language, religion, political or other opinion, national, ethnic or social origin, property, *disability,* birth or other status (Article 2) (emphasis added). Article 23 of the UNCRC is dedicated exclusively to children with disabilities, stating that 'a mentally or physically disabled child should enjoy a full and decent life, in conditions which ensure dignity, promote self-reliance and facilitate the child's active participation in the community.' Children with disabilities also have the right to participate in (early) education (Articles 28 and 29). This is restated in General Comment 7:

> Young children should never be institutionalized solely on the grounds of disability. It is a priority to ensure that they have equal opportunities to participate fully in education and community life, including by the removal of barriers that impede the realization of their rights.
>
> (United Nations Committee on the Rights of the Child, United Nations Children's Fund and Bernard van Leer Foundation, 2006)

The United Nations Convention on the Rights of Persons with Disabilities (CRPD), which came into force in May 2008, stresses the importance of early intervention as well as inclusion in the education system from an early age and states that children with disabilities must be able to 'access an inclusive, quality and free primary education and secondary education on an equal basis with others in the communities in which they live.' (United Nations 2006, CRPD, article 24).

The importance of inclusive educational provision is also highlighted in a recent UNESCO *Policy Brief on Early Childhood*, which argues that early childhood education and care is 'a powerful means of nurturing diverse abilities and overcoming disadvantages and inequalities' (UNESCO 2009).

Conventions such as the UNCRC and the CRPD are legally and morally binding for those governments who have ratified them. However, 20 years after the UNCRC came into force, progress in the actual implementation of the articles is described as being 'slow, but steady' (Krappmann 2009: 5). Progress in realizing child rights, including the rights of children with disabilities, is influenced by both the authority of the UNCRC and the efforts of civil societies, non-government agencies, researchers and practitioners. These interact and influence each other. Clearly social and cultural factors also play an important role in attitudes to children with disabilities and the extent to which they realize their rights to participate. How then can they be realized within the context of inclusive early childhood education and care?

What is inclusive education?

Schwartz *et al.* (2002) developed a list of key characteristics of inclusive programmes, consisting of programme philosophy, scheduling, curriculum and adult issues. With regard to the curriculum, the authors mention the following relevant characteristic: 'opportunities of peer interactions, with appropriate supports to promote success' (Schwarz *et al.* 2002).

Parents of children who have disabilities, as well as parents of children who are typically developing, are generally supportive of opportunities for pre-school inclusion, although some studies have identified important concerns. Rafferty and Griffin (2005) compared parents' perspectives on the benefits and risks associated with the inclusion of children with and without disabilities and pre-school providers in the same pre-school programme using two scales. Perceived benefits of including children with disabilities for children with disabilities were identified as: preparing disabled children to function effectively in the real world; enabling them to learn by observing typically developing children; providing them with more chances to participate in activities; and promoting community acceptance of children with disabilities. The perceived risks of inclusion for children with disabilities included: teachers not being qualified or trained for their needs; children being less likely to receive enough special help and/or individualized instruction from the teacher; and children being more likely to be rejected and/or left out by other children.

The perceived benefits of inclusion for typically developing children were identified as helping them to accept differences in people and sensitivity to others and becoming aware of their strengths and weaknesses. The perceived risks included the possibility of being injured by children with disabilities; of being frightened by unusual behaviour; that children with disabilities may slow down their learning; that they may not receive their fair share of materials and resources; difficulty in maintaining order in an inclusive classroom; and that they may learn negative behaviours. Most parents interviewed by Rafferty and Griffin (2005) agreed that inclusion provided children with disabilities with more chance to participate in activities and helped all children accept difference.

While parents and practitioners may broadly support the inclusion of disabled children, for inclusion to work and to be a positive experience for children in practice, extra planning and support are required and attention needs to be paid to supporting the development of an inclusive culture. The *Index for Inclusion* (Booth, Ainscow and Kingston 2006) is a practical resource on how to foster the development of play, learning and participation of *all* children, not limited to children with disabilities. The framework to improve inclusive settings consists of three dimensions:

1 creating inclusive cultures
2 producing inclusive policies
3 evolving inclusive practices

According to the authors, creating inclusive cultures lies at the heart of improvement of settings (Booth, Ainscow and Kingston 2006).

When it comes to understanding the processes and practicalities involved, it is important to recognize the diversity within the very broad category 'children with disabilities'. Children with disabilities are not a single homogeneous group and should not be considered as such. Important questions arise including what do we actually mean when we refer to disability? How does the seriousness and nature of a disability affect what is possible in inclusion? How does our understanding of disability influence our views about children's peer relations in inclusive settings?

Understandings of disability

Like 'inclusion', there is no universal definition of 'disability'. Understandings of disability can differ across settings, cultures and time. The International Classification of

Functioning, Disability and Health (ICF) views disability as an outcome of the interaction of the health conditions of a person and contextual factors, such as physical and attitudinal barriers (WHO 2002). This means that a 'disability' is not solely seen as a feature of a person (medical model), nor as a purely socially created problem (social model). The ICF combines these two models in an integrated *biopsychosocial* model (WHO 2002), which recognizes disability as the outcome of the interaction between features of a person and of the environment.

Although there is debate on how to define 'disability', children who have certain health conditions are often labelled as 'physically disabled', 'intellectually disabled', 'visually impaired', etc. Within these broad categories, there are many specifically identified disorders such as: cerebral palsy; movement disorders; epilepsy; Down's syndrome, communication disorders; autistic spectrum disorders; and attention deficit/hyperactivity disorder (ADHD). These classifications do not, however, give any information about the level of functioning of these children or about their level of participation in society. These are important concerns when considering children's peer relations.

What does research tell us about peer relationships and friendship in inclusive settings?

In tandem with formal early childhood settings becoming increasingly inclusive, there has been an increase in research on peer relationships and friendships among children with disabilities in early childhood and education settings. On the one hand friendships among children with disabilities do not seem to be different from friendships between typically developing children. For example, Dietrich (2005) carried out a qualitative study in the United States about friendship pairs among four preschool-aged children with disabilities (one child with a physical disability and three children with developmental delays) and four typically developing children in two inclusive settings. The friendships are described as 'typical' and have many of the characteristics of young children's friendships noted in other chapters of this book, such as 'being nice to one another, showing affection to each other, liking one another, choosing to spend time together and playing and having fun together' (Dietrich 2005: 206).

On the other hand, children with disabilities engage in social interactions with peers less often than typically developing children in inclusive classrooms (Odom 2000). Some studies in the United States indicate that children with disabilities are less preferred as playmates than typically developing peers (Guralnick 1999). However, it is important to remember that some typically developing children also have difficulties making friends.

Let us examine in more detail some of the factors that come into play. Webster and Carter (2007) identified 11 studies carried out in Western countries related to social relationships of very young children with developmental disabilities in early childhood education settings. Two important issues were identified by the authors. Firstly, very few studies focused on the relationships of children who had been exposed to inclusive settings over several years. Secondly, many studies focused on peer status and acceptance and did not necessarily measure the actual existence of friendship between children with disabilities and typical peers. Thus, there may be a discrepancy between peer acceptance and actual (reciprocated) friendship, which involves mutual preference and pro-social behaviour.

For example, a study by Dyson (2005) investigated young children's understanding of, and attitudes towards, disabilities. In this study, interviews were held with 77 children (aged five to six years) enrolled in inclusive classrooms in Canada. An overwhelming majority of children (84 per cent) answered positively to the question: 'Do you like people who have disabilities or have special needs?' However, less than half of the children (47 per cent) reported having friends with disabilities.

This finding is also reflected in a study that examined the social preferences of children who are developing typically towards children with disabilities in four pre-school classes in the United States (Nabors 1997). The children were asked to nominate three classmates they liked to play with and three classmates they did not like to play with. Children with disabilities received fewer positive nominations than expected based on their representation in each of the classrooms in three classes, but did not receive more negative nominations. Thus children with special needs may be neglected by their non-disabled peers, but not altogether rejected. The children who were disliked by their classmates were perceived as aggressive irrespective of disability status (Nabors 1997).

However, when Hestenes and Carroll (2000) interviewed 21 typically developing children (between the ages of three years and four months and seven years and four months) in the United States to assess the children's preference of playing with their peers with or without disabilities, there were no differences in typically developing children's preferences to play with peers without disabilities compared to peers with disabilities. In this study children sorted pictures of their classmates into three boxes representing 'I like to play with him/her a lot', 'I sometimes like to play with her' and 'I do not like to play with him/her very much'.

One of the questions explored in inclusion studies is whether or not children's familiarity and information about disabilities has an impact on peer relations and friendship formation. In Hestenes and Carroll's (2000) study children were also shown three dolls to assess their overall understanding of disability. One doll represented a child with a physical disability, one doll represented a child with a visual disability and one doll did not have a disability. The children were asked to rate how well each doll might perform on tasks that involved different abilities. The study found that children's preference to play with peers with disabilities was significantly predicted by their understanding of disability.

Okagaki *et al.* (1998) used similar dolls to assess children's ideas about children with disabilities in general. They found that children's attitudes towards peers with disabilities were positively related to the frequency of children's actual contact with classmates with disabilities during free play time. However, when Hestenes and Carroll (2000) studied young children's actual play interactions in inclusive pre-schools settings, they found that typically developing children spent less time interacting with their peers with disabilities. Actual interactions with peers were predicted by children's age and their teacher's presence, not by their understanding of disability or playmate preference, as assessed by children's nomination.

To summarize: firstly there may be a difference in what children say and do; secondly, children with disabilities may be more often neglected but not necessarily rejected play partners; and thirdly, the amount of actual contact between children with disabilities and non-disabled peers, i.e. time spent together, and the number of children with disabilities in the setting also impact on peer relationships in inclusive settings.

Challenges to peer relationships and friendship

When considering the actual experience of friendship it is also worth considering 'softer' related characteristics of friendship that have been identified as significant in children's peer culture but which are more difficult to measure, such as feelings of belonging, connectedness or togetherness. These are closely linked with the experience of jointly doing, thinking or expressing something, or physically acting together in play. As noted in Chapter 3 of this book, togetherness and coordination in play require sophisticated verbal, social and physical skills. What are the experiences and challenges of children with different kinds of disabilities in this regard?

Wolfberg *et al.*'s (1999) research in the United States investigated the experiences of ten children presenting significant developmental delays or disabilities and their non-disabled classmates in six pre-school programmes for children aged four to six years. In this study, Wolfberg found that every child with disabilities expressed a desire to participate in peer culture, albeit sometimes in unconventional ways. For example, one child with Down's syndrome approached her peers by watching, following and occasionally imitating their actions to express her desire to play with them.

A second finding was that every child with a disability experienced inclusion in peer culture in one form or another. The researchers observed a variety of ways and situations in which disabled children participated in peer cultural activities. Establishing common ground (such as a mutual interest) offered children a way to coordinate activities and, in some cases, develop a mutual friendship. They described how one child with autism shared a mutual interest with his peers in the Disney film *The Lion King*. When the music played on the tape recorder, he joined the other children in song and dance.

Finally, the majority of children with disabilities experienced exclusion from their peer culture in some fashion. At least one half of the children with disabilities had experienced apathy and indifference from their typically developing peers. For example, the author describes how when a child with Down's syndrome goes to the play area and looks around for someone to play with, she is ignored by the other children and remains alone. Wolfberg found that other factors impeding peer relations included 'misinterpreting and overlooking social cues', 'conflict over space and property' and 'tittle-tales, gossips and cliques' (Wolfberg *et al.* 1999: 80).

Similarly, a Swedish study of togetherness between visually impaired and sighted pre-school children (Janson 2001) draws attention to how the related factors of access to physical space, ability to engage in social interaction and engage in symbolic play can all have a bearing on children's experience of togetherness and friendship. The transcribed play negotiations between children serve to illustrate how differences in visual ability can impede togetherness:

In the following episode Pia, blind, is the driver of the train; the train consists of chairs in a row. She stands behind the first chair, supposed to be the railway engine. Anna, a sighted passenger, is sitting on another chair. Pia makes 'train noises'.

PIA: 'Now the train is running'.
ANNA: 'No it isn't. First you must sit on your chair in the engine.'
PIA: 'Not me.'
ANNA: 'Yes, you must.'
... (YES-AND-NO QUARRELING FOR SOME TIME.)
T: 'Let's say the train has an auto-pilot, just press a button and the train runs by itself.'
PIA: (Pretends to press a button.) 'Now the train is running.'
ANNA: 'It isn't. I can see it isn't.'
PIA: (Moves herself in small circles beside the engine chair.) 'Now it's running.'
ANNA: 'I know it isn't. I know that.'
PIA: 'Now I press it again, now it stops.' (Repeating circling movements.) 'Now it runs.'
ANNA: 'It isn't.'

(Janson 2001: 140–141)

This episode is about two conflicting ideas about what constitutes train movement. To Anna, it is necessary to sit in the driver's seat to drive the train. To Pia, driving a train is about making 'train movements'. In this case, differences in representation have resulted in conflict. According to Janson (2001) the conflict cannot be attributed to the individual characteristics of the children, but differences in the apprehension of the situation: 'All participants, blind as well as sighted, demonstrate limited ability, i.e. disability, in embracing the meaning of each other's proposals' (Janson 2001:142).

Harper and McCluskey (2002) conclude that children with communication difficulties are at particular risk of social isolation. They compared the free-play social behaviours of 24 children with language and motor disabilities in inclusive pre-school programmes with their non-disabled classmates in the United States. Children who used little or no productive language spent more time in solitary pursuits and seldom initiated interactions. Similarly, children who were incapable of independent locomotion were largely dependent on adults for initiating social exchanges. These findings raise a number of important implications for practice.

Implications for practice

Good practice in early childhood education requires adults paying attention to both commonalities and similarities with a group as well as acknowledging differences. This also applies when promoting peer relationships and friendships in inclusive settings. General strategies that apply to all groups with young children also have relevance when addressing the needs of children in inclusive settings. These include the provision of sufficient time for free play for the development of friendships; arranging the physical space indoors and outdoors to facilitate both small group and larger group interaction; allowing noisy, silly, active play so that children can have fun and experience the togetherness that comes from shared laughter; keeping friends together in the same group; and practitioners and parents sharing information about shared interests between children and possible emerging friendships (Goldman and Buysse 2007; see also Chapter 3 this volume).

A number of additional strategies need particular attention for successful inclusion of children with disabilities in peer cultures. These necessitate planning in advance of inclusion, careful observation and monitoring of children's experiences and the effects of adult interventions, and good teamwork between all those involved: parents, practitioners and support staff. It is also important to recognize children as a resource in their capacity to help and support each other. Let us examine a number of specific recommendations. For children with physical disabilities, some modifications to the physical environment will enhance participation. Examples include: the provision of ramps, railings (Jinnah-Ghelani and Stoneman 2009) and wheeled toys that encourage cooperation. Insley and Lucas (2009) highlight the importance of good communication between adults working together to support children who are vulnerable to exclusion as a result of social, emotional and behavioural difficulties. Here, the verbal and non-verbal interaction between the teaching team (teacher and individual support assistant or classroom assistant) can work as a model for children of positive interaction, empathy, resolving conflicts, sharing pleasure, enjoyment and humour (Insley and Lucas 2009: 163). Teachers may also need to act as social–cultural interpreters and guides when helping children respond to cues, establish common ground and normalize unconventional behaviour (Wolfberg *et al.* 1999).

Children with disabilities gain confidence through participation in activities they can be successful in. The term 'accommodation' is used to refer to the changes that are made in how a child with a disability has access to the curriculum or demonstrate learning in order for this to be possible (Batshaw Clair *et al.* 2007). Often the focus is on cognitive and academic skills. However, it is also important that social and friendship skills are recognized as a valuable part of the curricula. Adults can help non-disabled children make appropriate accommodations during play with disabled children, in order that play can continue (Hestenes and Carroll 2000).

Finally, as discussed earlier in this chapter, the provision of information to parents and non-disabled children may also contribute to the promotion of a non-judgemental, accepting and inclusive attitude within a group. All of these strategies require that practitioners are sufficiently trained and receive ongoing support and mentoring in their work with young disabled children and their families.

Concluding comments

A child rights approach to early childhood education and care offers a firm foundation for policy, as it recognizes that 'children are social actors, entitled to respect, care, education and comprehensive services in their best interests' (Woodhead 2009). The adoption of the UN CRPD coupled with specific articles in the UNCRC and

General Comment 7 relating to children with disabilities draw governments' attention to the particular needs and rights of this group. While these are important advocacy tools, it is also acknowledged that there is huge variation across countries regarding the extent to which they are upheld in practice. Research cited in this chapter indicates that children with disabilities often face barriers to play and participation, although there are inconsistent findings regarding whether or not children with disabilities interact less often with other children than their typically developing peers in inclusive settings.

Having friends is beneficial for all children. To be able to promote friendship between children with disabilities and their typically developing peers, children with disabilities first of all need to be included in early childhood education settings instead of being placed in separate settings. However, an 'inclusive' setting is no guarantee that children with disabilities are included in the 'peer culture' (Wolfberg *et al.* 1999). By sharing knowledge and experience, practitioners and parents can do a lot to promote peer relationships and friendship between children with and without disabilities.

Finally, we would like to stress, as Odom (2000) does, that 'inclusion' goes far beyond the classroom. Inclusive early childhood services should not be seen as an end in itself, rather as a means to prepare children with disabilities for life in the wider community. It also means that all children can experience diversity as a routine part of life. Children with disabilities have a right to be included in society and we, as adults, have the obligation to respect, promote and fulfil this right.

Acknowledgement

Thanks are due to Annabel Trapp, ICDI for her helpful comments and suggestions on an earlier draft of this chapter.

Point for reflection and discussion

In this chapter von der Assen and Kernan present a viewpoint, based on human rights principles, that all children have an equal right to participate in inclusive settings where they can develop peer relationships. Is that a viewpoint that is common in your region? Think of an early years setting you know. How can barriers to play and peer relationships for children with disabilities be minimized and how can friendships between children be encouraged?

Note

1 Nina von der Assen works with Margaret Kernan at International Child Development Initiatives (ICDI), Leiden, the Netherlands. ICDI is an international non-governmental organization, which works to promote the well-being of children growing up in difficult circumstances by assisting in the development of local capacity (of children, their communities, organizations and authorities) to improve policies and practices. Nina's expertise includes children with disabilities and children's rights.

Bibliography

Batshaw Clair, E., Church, R.P. and Batshaw, M.L. (2007) 'Special education services'. In M.L. Batshaw, L. Pellegrino and N.L. Roizon (eds) *Children with Disabilities*, 6th edition. Baltimore, M.D.: Paul H. Brookes.

Booth, T., Ainscow, M. and Kingston, D. (2006) *Index for Inclusion: Developing Play, Learning and Participation in Early Years and Childcare*. Centre for Studies on Inclusive Education. www.eenet.org.uk/resources/docs/Index%20EY%20English.pdf (accessed 16 November 2009).

Committee on the Rights of the Child (2005) *General Comment 7: Implementing Child Rights in Early Childhood*. www2.ohchr.org/english/bodies/crc/docs/AdvanceVersions/GeneralComment7Rev1.pdf (accessed 26 October 2009).

——(2006) *General Comment 9: The Rights of Children with Disabilities*. www.unhchr.ch/tbs/doc.nsf/898586b1dc7b4043c1256a450044f331/405ba882cb9eb3a0c12572f100506ac4/$FILE/G0740702.pdf (accessed 26 October 2009).

Diamond, K.E., Hong, S. and Tu, H. (2008) 'Context influences preschool children's decisions to include a peer with a physical disability in play'. *Exceptionality*, 16(3): 141–55.

Dietrich, S.L. (2005) 'A look at friendships between preschool-aged children with and without disabilities in two inclusive classrooms'. *Journal of Early Childhood Research*, 3: 193–215.

Dyson, L.L. (2005) 'Kindergarten children's understanding of and attitudes toward people with disabilities'. *Topics in Early Childhood Special Education*, 25(2): 95–105.

Goldman, B.D. and Buysse, V. (2007) 'Friendships in very young children'. In O. Saracho and B. Spodek (eds) *Contemporary Perspectives on Research in Socialization and Social Development*. Charlotte, N.C.: Information Age Publishing,

Guralnick, M.J. (1999) 'The nature and meaning of social integration for young children with mild developmental delays in inclusive settings'. *Journal of Early Intervention*, 22(1): 70–86.

Harper, L.V. and McCluskey, K.S. (2002) 'Caregiver and peer responses to children with language and motor disabilities in inclusive preschool programs'. *Early Childhood Research Quarterly*, 17:148–66.

Hestenes, L.L. and Carroll, D.E. (2000) 'The play interactions of young children with and without disabilities: individual and environmental influences'. *Early Childhood Research Quarterly*, 15(2): 229–46.

Insley, K. and Lucas, S. (2009) 'Making the most of the relationship between two adults to impact on early childhood education'. In T. Papatheodorou and J. Moyles (eds) *Learning Together in the Early Years: Exploring Relational Pedagogy*. Abingdon: Routledge.

Janson, U. (2001) 'Togetherness and diversity in pre-school play'. *International Journal of Early Years Education*, 9(2): 134–43.

Jinnah-Ghelani, H.A. and Stoneman, Z. (2009) 'Elements of successful inclusion for school-age children with disabilities in childcare setting'. *Childcare in Practice*, 15(3): 175–91.

Krappmann, L. (2009) 'Slow, but steady progress', an interview with Lothar Krappmann. *Early Childhood Matters*, 113. The Hague: Bernard van Leer Foundation.

Nabors. L. (1997) 'Playmate preferences of children who are typically developing for their classmates with special needs'. *Mental Retardation*, 35(20): 107–13.

Odom, S.L. (2000) 'Preschool inclusion: what we know and where we go from here'. *Topics in Early Childhood Special Education*, 20(1): 20–7.

Odom, S.L. (ed) (2002) *Widening the Circle: Including Children with Disabilities in Preschool Programs*. New York: Teachers College Press.

Okagaki, L., Diamond, K.E., Kontos, S.J. and Hestenes, L.L. (1998) 'Correlates of young children's interactions with classmates with disabilities'. *Early Childhood Research Quarterly*, 13(1): 67–86.

Rafferty, Y. and Griffin, K.W. (2005) 'Benefits and risks of reverse inclusion for preschoolers with and without disabilities: perspectives of parents and providers'. *Journal of Early Intervention*, 27(3): 173–92.

Schwartz, I.S., Sandall, S.R., Odom. S.L., Horn, E. and Beckman, P.J. (2002) 'I know it when I see it: in search of a common definition of inclusion.' In Odom, S.L. (ed) *Widening the Circle: Including Children with Disabilities in Preschool Programs*. New York: Teachers College Press.

United Nations (1989) *UN Convention on the Rights of the Child*. Geneva, UN. www2.ohchr.org/english/law/pdf/crc.pdf (accessed 26 October 2009).

——(2006) *UN Convention on the Rights of Persons with Disabilities*. Geneva, UN. www.un.org/disabilities/documents/convention/convoptprot-e.pdf (accessed 26 October 2009).

United Nations Committee on the Rights of the Child, United Nations Children's Fund and Bernard van Leer Foundation (2006) *A Guide to General Comment 7: 'Implementing Child Rights in Early Childhood'*. The Hague: Bernard van Leer Foundation.

UNESCO (2009) *UNESCO Policy Brief on Early Childhood. Inclusion of Children with Disabilities: the Early Childhood Imperative*. No. 46, April–June 2009/REV.

Webster, A.A. and Carter, M. (2007) 'Social relationships and friendships of children with developmental disabilities: implications for inclusive settings. A systematic review'. *Journal of Intellectual & Developmental Disability*, 32(3): 200–13.

Wolfberg, P.J., Zercher, C., Lieber, J. *et al.* (1999) '"Can I play with you?" Peer culture in inclusive preschool programs'. *Journal of the Association for Persons with Severe Handicaps*, 24: 69–84.

Woodhead, M. (2009) 'The rights of the child case'. In I. Siraj-Blatchford and M. Woodhead (eds) *Effective Early Childhood Programme: Early Childhood in Focus 4*. Milton Keynes: The Open University.

WHO (2002) *Towards a Common Language for Functioning, Disability and Health. ICF*. www.who.int/classifications/icf/training/icfbeginnersguide.pdf (accessed 26 October 2009).

Chapter 10

Training early years practitioners to support young children's social relationships

Miriam Rosenthal and Lihi Gatt[1]

Introduction

This chapter describes a training programme, Learning to Live Together (LtLT), developed in Israel for caregivers working with toddlers and pre-schoolers in childcare settings. The programme aims at articulating the role of the early childhood educator as a facilitator of socio-emotional competence of very young children. Participants in the programme learn how to transform the childcare setting into an environment in which children may acquire patterns of considerate, respectful and empathetic interpersonal relations. The programme was initially developed for untrained caregivers working with infants and toddlers in centre-based daycare or family daycare. It has also been disseminated for years to directors and supervisors of childcare settings as well as to coordinators and supervisors of intervention programmes for disadvantaged children.

The context of daycare in Israel

As is the case in many other countries, the daycare system serving children under three years old in Israel is very different from the one serving pre-schoolers (aged three to six years). The two systems have different goals and different ministries set their policies. Pre-school for three- to six-year-old children comes under the jurisdiction of the Ministry of Education. All teachers are required to have college-based training in early childhood education. The system serves approximately 90 per cent of Israeli children. Daycare for zero- to three-year-old children comes under the jurisdiction of the Ministry of Industry, Commerce and Employment. The major goal of this ministry is to encourage mothers of very young children to join the labour market. Hence, the emphasis is on offering a safe and healthy environment for children. The system's secondary goal is to serve at-risk children in poor and/or immigrant families. Full- or half-day daycare is used by many parents for their very young children, partly because in many young families both parents are working and partly because many Israeli mothers believe their young children 'enjoy being in the company of other children'.

Many Israeli infants and toddlers may spend eight hours a day, five to six days a week, in out-of-home childcare. Most childcare settings in Israel are characterized by very large groups (18–27 infants; 30–35 toddlers), and poor adult:child ratios (about 3:24 in infants groups; 3:34 with older toddlers). Most caregivers have no training, and only ten to twelve years of education. The working conditions of the caregivers are very poor, resulting in observed poor emotional climate and low-quality adult–child interactions, such as ignoring children's distress and occasional offensive behaviour towards children (Rosenthal 1991, 1994; Koren-Karie *et al.* 1998). This results in a high frequency of conflicts and violent interaction among children (Furman 1994).

Caregivers in family daycare also tend to ignore children's conflicts and emotional distress. As a result, children spend more time being emotionally distressed and have less time in positive interaction with their peers (Rosenthal and Zur 1993).

Interview studies with Israeli caregivers highlighted the stress experienced daily by these hardworking women. Caregivers find themselves navigating daily in a complex environment characterized by an abundance of highly stressed relationships: strained adult–child relations, adult–adult relations and child–child relations (Gatt 2008). These women are metaphorically 'putting out fires' while trying to meet everyone's needs and demands, knowing they cannot serve the 'best interest' of the children in their care ('I am glad I survived another day') (Zadok 2005). In-service training, when offered to the caregivers, in most Israeli daycare settings focuses on cognitively oriented activities. Socio-emotional issues are overlooked, and as a result most educators working with very young children are poorly prepared for their role of supporting the development of early socio-emotional competence (Gatt 2008).

The situation in Israeli daycare settings raises a serious concern for the social and emotional development and well-being of children in group settings. Therefore there is a need to train staff in daycare settings to use the group context as an opportunity to help children develop social and emotional capabilities. The LtLT programme concentrates on the active role of the caregiver as a *facilitator* of socio-emotional competence of children, and on his/her responsibility for the emotional climate in the childcare setting.

Attachment is not enough

For years, attachment theory has dominated most explanations of socio-emotional development in the early years. Attachment theory would suggest that to promote children's socio-emotional competence, the caregiver should 'sensitively respond' to children as individuals, thus creating a 'secure base' for every child in the group. Indeed, many studies have found that more sensitive and responsive behaviour by caregivers was associated with less negative, and more positive play with other children, over and above the influence of child and family characteristics (Howes 2000; NICHD 2001). Other studies, however, suggest that not all caregivers who promote positive, secure relationships with the toddlers in their care do necessarily encourage or support positive peer interaction (Howes *et al.* 1994). The latter imply that caregivers in whose care children have positive peer interaction, must be doing other things besides responding sensitively to children.

Our argument is that attachment theory and its focus on general behaviour categories such as 'warmth' or 'sensitive responsiveness', is limited in its ability to explain the impact caregivers may have on children's developing socio-emotional competence in a group setting. Firstly, it ignores the fact that some specific behaviours included in the general category of 'sensitive responsiveness' may have different effects on different social and emotional behaviours of children. Thus, for example, soothing and comforting children during moments of distress might be more effective in promoting their emotion regulation and empathic response to others than caregivers' general positive responsiveness and expressions of warmth and positive feelings towards them (Davidov and Grusec 2006). But soothing and comforting behaviour of the caregiver does not necessarily mean that it will also affect children's level of play with peers.

Our second argument is that attachment theory ignores the social learning opportunities offered by the group setting of childcare. The group setting is discussed usually in terms of the limits it sets on the educator's ability to respond sensitively to each individual child. But the attachment theory ignores the rich social and emotional learning opportunities provided to children by other children in the group and by observing and witnessing emotional and social events of others in the group.

When it comes to training, therefore, we suggest that the general instruction to caregivers to 'respond sensitively' to children is not enough to help them support the

Source: Copyright Barbara Rosenstein/Bernard van Leer Foundation

socio-emotional development of very young children in group care. Caregivers ought to be trained in the use of a variety of specific interventions during various daily emotional and social events that occur in the group among children, events that serve as opportunities of socio-emotional learning for young children.

The Learning to Live Together programme: goals and content

Based on this argument, the LtLT programme sets four major goals in the training of early years practitioners: (1) it offers research-based knowledge on socio-emotional development in the early years; (2) it teaches participants to identify daily 'learning opportunities' for promoting social competence in group settings; (3) it helps caregivers and educators acquire specific intervention skills; and (4) it encourages them to examine and clarify personal and culture-based attitudes and beliefs concerning early social and emotional development.

Empirical knowledge concerning toddlers' developing socio-emotional skills

The programme reviews for its participants the rich research literature on early development of emotion regulation, emotional understanding and early social communication skills. These include the different ways in which very young children communicate their feelings, wishes and intentions; infants' and toddlers' use of cues from adults to guide their emotional responses ('social referencing'); the manner by which they join and maintain a play interaction with other children; beginning inhibitory control and anger management skills; as well as the ways by which young children offer help and comfort to a distressed friend and share their possessions with others.

Furthermore, the training highlights young children's experiences in a group context and the effect of these experiences on their social behaviour and development. The participants are sensitized to individual differences among children and to the fact that the group situation might be more stressful for some children than for others (Rosenthal *et al.* 2008; Rosenthal and Gatt, in press).

Daily experiences in daycare as 'learning opportunities'

The LtLT programme teaches caregivers to identify the daily events in daycare that present 'learning opportunities' for promoting social and emotional competence. The daily events that are most frequently discussed are: moments of crying and other behaviours signalling children's distress; episodes of conflicts and acts of aggression; children's joint activities and unsuccessful attempts to join others in play; infants' and toddlers' expression of interest in a peer; as well as children's expression of concern for others and engagement in caring behaviour. The caregivers learn how they may use these daily experiences to help children develop emotion regulation and self-control, to

Source: Copyright Barbara Rosenstein/Bernard van Leer Foundation

promote children's social cognition and emotional understanding, to enhance communication and group entry skills, as well as acquire pro-social behaviour.

Early group experience: the 'audience phenomenon'

The LtLT training aims at alerting the caregivers to the fact that children in the group also learn from being an 'audience' to interactions among others. Throughout the day they listen and watch very intently the emotional expressions of others. They observe the different social exchanges between children, and mostly, they observe the exchanges between adults and other children. They observe and learn from how others regulate their emotions, or help each other in such regulation, and they learn from how others initiate interaction or respond to bids for joint attention, etc.

This understanding of the 'audience phenomenon' helps the participants of the LtLT programme appreciate the fact that the experience of any individual child in group care is always a 'social affair' and may serve as a 'learning opportunity'. Wherever there is an audience – there is always an actor. The training emphasizes the role of the caregiver as the key actor, the director and at times also the playwright and the stage manager of emotional and social events at daycare.

Moments of heightened emotionality in the group provide caregivers with rich opportunities for sustaining the 'audience's' attention. These include episodes of children crying or otherwise expressing distress, episodes of heightened jubilant expression, as well as episodes of social interaction charged with anger – between children, between adults and children, and between adults. These episodes of heightened emotionality offer moments of 'hot cognition', meaning that whatever is learned during moments of heightened emotions is retained well in one's memory (Hoffman 1984).

The 'theatre metaphor', and the understanding that an 'audience' of young children is always there, observing and learning throughout the day, has a great impact on the way caregivers perceive their crucial role vis-à-vis children's social and emotional learning. This metaphor, together with the understanding of the importance of moments of 'hot cognition', paves the way for a change in the behaviour of the caregivers in the LtLT training.

Specific behaviours that promote socio-emotional competence of young children in a group context

Research derived from social learning theories highlights some effective learning that occurs when adults 'model' to children specific behaviours or interactions; when adults 'coach' a child in some specific ways; and when they 'react contingently' to the child's behaviour (Denham 1998; Denham *et al.* 2003; Dunn 2000). Others highlight the importance of an adult 'attributing ability' to the child (Grusec and Redler 1980).

Throughout the training, caregivers acquire and practise specific behaviours within these general categories. Thus, for example, when a caregiver strives to remain calm during an emotionally charged situation she models emotion regulation. When, in addition, she soothes and comforts an upset child, she is reacting contingently to the distress (i.e. immediately following the child's expression), while at the same time she models to her audience a 'caring-for-other' behaviour. When she explains to the children the cause for the displayed emotion, or suggests to a child an alternative way of communicating his or her intent, she is coaching the 'target child' as well as the children in the 'audience'. When she suggests that a child 'talk to his little hands and remind them not to hit', or reminds children to 'be gentle', she implicitly conveys her trust in their ability of self-control.

The programme refers to these behaviours and interventions as the 'professional tool box' of the caregiver. The caregivers are encouraged to explore ways of explaining to children the emotion expressed during a given situation, its possible reasons and different ways of relating to it. They may encourage children to offer their own explanations for the emotion, or social behaviour, of a peer. The caregivers become aware of great individual differences among the children in their care, and are encouraged to give special attention to the needs of shy or withdrawn children, as well as to the so-called 'aggressive' children who might have especially poor skills of joining others in their play or poor inhibitory control.

During conflicts the caregivers are encouraged to coach children to use short but assertive verbal communication, or attribute regulatory abilities, as well as positive intentions ('Oops, I think you forgot to guard your hands today. I know you can!').

Caregivers also learn to recognize behaviours that do not support children's evolving socio-emotional competence. For example, ignoring children's emotional arousal or ridiculing a child's expression of emotion ('you are a silly cry-baby'); being impatient with an upset child, scolding, shouting or otherwise hurting the child. The caregivers are further encouraged to practise their newly acquired specific behaviours and interventions, and observe how this affects children's social and emotional behaviour as well as the emotional climate in the group.

Exploring cultural beliefs and personal attitudes of caregivers

The LtLT programme acknowledges the important effect culture-based beliefs and personal attitudes have on caregivers' behaviour and their interactions with children. We know from many studies that different cultures sustain different notions as to what is a 'socially and emotionally competent child' (Greenfield *et al.* 2003; Harkness and Super 1996) and consequently construct different socializing experiences for their children during the early childhood period. Therefore the programme encourages exploration and discussion of attitudes and beliefs caregivers hold concerning the ideal of a 'well-behaved' sociable child, and the best way to socialize children towards that goal. Training also explores the attitudes and beliefs of the caregivers regarding their own role and responsibility (other than that of parents) in supporting this development (Zur 2002).

The LtLT programme gives ample room for discussion of the participants' attitudes and beliefs. Both overt and covert attitudes and beliefs are triggered through video observation and various group exercises. Caregivers in the programme are challenged to articulate some of their conflicting values and ambivalence. This enables them to understand the 'double messages' they sometimes convey to children. For example, is a child who hits another child when fighting over a toy, being 'aggressive' or is he assertively defending his 'individual rights'? Is being empathetic and considerate towards other children a sign of social competence, or of a weakness ('being a sissy') that endangers the child's social position in the group? Is the frequent empathic responsiveness of a caregiver to a child in distress likely to make him 'securely attached' or 'manipulative'? In addition to conflicting attitudes each caregiver may experience *within* him/herself, these discussions may also highlight differences in values held by different staff members coming from different cultural backgrounds.

The exploration of caregivers' attitudes and beliefs is of special importance in multicultural societies. Israeli caregivers come from a variety of cultural backgrounds. Many come from immigrant families from Arab countries, such as Morocco or Iraq, and from the former USSR, and Ethiopia. Some are religiously orthodox while others are secular, some are Arabs and some are Jewish. Attitudes and cultural values related to social and emotional behaviours have to be sensitively dealt with in the programme.

Learning to Live Together: method of training

The training programme has two parts: the first consists of 12 bi-monthly group meetings in the format of workshops, guided by an early childhood expert. The second part takes the format of four bi-monthly consultation meetings in small groups, analyzing video-observation of challenging children from the caregivers' group.

Part I: the workshops

The 12 bi-monthly meetings are conducted as discussion groups, and make use of exciting group exercises and video vignettes to trigger off the discussion. The empirically-based knowledge of children's development and daily learning opportunities, as well as of the knowledge concerning caregivers' behaviour that promotes socio-emotional competence, is introduced throughout these discussions in an experiential, non-academic manner.

The group facilitator uses a guidebook (Gatt 2004) and a series of three short training films (Gatt 1999) developed exclusively for this programme. Furthermore, events occurring 'here and now' during the workshops are utilized to highlight the emotional and social skills required by adults, as well as by children, to participate and adjust to a group experience. The caregivers are encouraged to try out different competence promoting interventions in their daily work with children and report back to the group about their impact on children's emotional and social interactions. Most importantly, the group discussions provide ample opportunities to examine different attitudes and beliefs, and allow the participants to share their personal life experiences (memories of childhood, raising one's children and group experiences as adults) as well as draw on their experience of working with young children in groups.

The content of the workshops is organized as four units: (1) Understanding young children's group experience; (2) Toddlers learn empathy; (3) Toddlers learn to play together; and (4) Toddlers learn to resolve conflicts.

The first unit – Understanding young children's group experience – discusses daily challenges faced by a young child during his or her long hours in a group situation with his or her peers. The main message is that although groups of young children have their own unique characteristics, adults encounter similar experiences in groups, and can identify with the difficulties and challenges that children encounter. The caregivers draw on their own immediate experience in the workshop in order to explore similarities and differences with the group experience of very young children, and pinpoint the skills needed for group participation.

The second unit – Toddlers learn empathy – focuses on children's expression of distress, and their attentiveness to each others' emotions when in group care. Moreover, the participants learn to identify subtle expressions of concern and empathy of children as well as their budding pro-social attempts to help or soothe the upset child. The discussions of this topic focus on knowledge and attitudes concerning (a) young children's understanding of emotion, and the teacher's role in toddlers' 'social referencing'; (b) the effectiveness of learning that takes place during moments of heightened emotionality ('hot cognition'); (c) the relationship between emotion regulation and toddlers' ability to engage in empathic behaviour; as well as (d) children's competent empathic behaviour and its effect on leadership and popularity in the group.

The discussions of caregivers' behaviour ('professional tool box') highlight the fact that the caregiver's comforting behaviours and his/her emotional discourse during moments of distress and heightened emotionality in the group serve multiple functions: (a) they comfort the upset child, helping him/her to regulate his/her emotions; (b) they help children in the 'audience' regulate their emotions, and understand their peer's emotions, thus enabling them to attend to the needs of their peer; and also (c) while engaging in these behaviours the caregiver serves as an empathic model to his/her 'audience' of children (d) altogether, through his/her behaviour, the teacher generates the needed supportive emotional climate that encourages pro-social behaviour among children in the group.

The third unit – Toddlers learn to play together – includes discussions of toddlers' developing skills of perspective taking, social understanding, as well as of their budding communication competence and the importance of these skills for a child's participation in group life. The discussions sensitize the caregivers to subtle cues and signals of toddlers expressing interest in each other's play, and their rather limited skills of initiating interaction with others in the group. They further draw attention to toddlers' effortful attempts to understand the intent of a peer who expresses interest in what they do or in their play object. Many caregivers and teachers believe it is inappropriate to 'intervene' or 'interfere' in children's play. The workshops allow for discussions of these beliefs. Through these discussions the caregivers learn to appreciate the need to guide young children in their social play interactions, and the significant difference between 'guiding' and 'interfering'. Furthermore, they learn to appreciate that their interventions are especially important for shy, inhibited or withdrawn children, or for children whose communication skills are still very limited. Also, many caregivers and teachers express a negative attitude towards exuberant, imitative, joint-play. They describe this form of play as 'wild', unaware of its importance for the evolving 'peer culture' and children's social development.

The discussion of caregivers' behaviour ('professional tool box') focus on the role of the educator in 'igniting interactions' among peers, and scaffolding children's emerging social skills, through helping them acquire unambiguous communication skills to indicate to others their wish to play together, as well as through teaching children how they can find out the intentions and wishes of others.

The fourth unit – Toddlers learn to resolve conflicts – discusses the way young children handle their disagreements. The participants learn to distinguish between 'conflicts' and 'aggression' or 'violence', to identify typical conflicts among toddlers and understand their developmental roots. They learn also to appreciate the different characteristics of toddlers' strategies of coping with anger and frustration.

Caregivers are encouraged to serve as 'co-regulators' to a child going through an arousing experience of conflict. They learn to address the intentions, wishes and needs of both children engaged in conflict, and serve as 'mediators', not as judges of, or advocates for, one party. Caregivers are also trained to coach children in the use of alternative assertive, prosocial strategies while attributing to them innate regulatory abilities, as well as positive intentions, even when a child has acted in an antisocial way towards his peer.

Throughout all four units, caregivers are also encouraged to generate social and emotional learning through planned activities – such as 'story telling' or a 'puppet show', which feature social-interaction situations and emotional episodes.

Part 2: the consultation meetings

The second stage of the LtLT training offers consultation meetings in small groups, which typically include the staff working in one class in the childcare centre, where all the caregivers are familiar with the children in the group. These meetings allow the caregivers to focus on children exhibiting low social competence with challenging social and emotional behaviour (i.e. those having trouble adjusting to group care, exhibiting internalizing (shy or withdrawn) behaviour, as well as heightened externalizing behaviour, such as overt expression of anger, aggression, excessive crying or other negative emotions and/or social behaviour). Similar to the first part, this second part of the training programme is also held away from the classroom, after working hours, when the caregivers are free to contemplate and reflect on their work.

These meetings are based on the 'video-aided supervision' training model developed at the Hebrew University in Jerusalem (Gatt 2005, 2008). Using a small camcorder, a target child is filmed by the caregiver during daily activity at daycare. The video observations of these vignettes sensitize the caregivers to individual children, facilitating a process of deep viewing and tuning into each child's daily group experience. A dynamic process of observation occurs as the caregivers view the tapes again and again, thus gaining new insights into the child's overt behaviour and covert intentions, identifying his/her subtle gestures and acknowledging his/her unique communicative pattern.

The caregivers typically choose to film children that present some social or emotional problem such as socially withdrawn, isolated or aggressive children. Yet, at the same time, these consultation meetings deepen the participants' understanding of children in general, and reinforce the use of the specific intervention skills acquired during the workshops.

Evaluation of the programme

The effectiveness of the LtLT programme was systematically assessed using a classical 'before-and-after' design (Beer 2007).

Sample

Eighty-two caregivers working in 12 daycare centres participated in the study: 44 worked with young toddlers (15–24 months old), 38 worked with older toddlers (24–36 months old). The sample was divided into two groups – an 'intervention group' that participated in the LtLT training (40 caregivers in six daycare centres), and a 'control group' that received other training offered by the childcare organization (42 caregivers in six other daycare centres). All 12 centres had the same structural characteristics of large group-size, poor adult:child ratio and very low caregivers' education and training level. In addition, 78 children (39 boys and 39 girls) participated in the study, 38 in the 'intervention group' and 40 in the 'control group'.

Measures

Measures were taken at the beginning of the school year and immediately at the end of the training. These included an assessment of (1) caregivers' behaviour; (2) overall quality; and (3) children's behaviour, with the help of standardized observation scales.

Summary of results and conclusions

Following the intervention, caregivers who participated in the LtLT training were significantly more likely than caregivers in the control group to offer verbal and emotional support to children during moments of emotional arousal, such as moments of crying or conflicts. They also engaged more frequently in behaviours that promote conflict resolution skills and group-entry skills.

The differences between the intervention and the control groups were much more pronounced among caregivers working with older toddlers (24–36 months old) than among those working with younger toddlers (15–24 months old). The caregivers of older children in the intervention group expressed significantly greater warmth towards the children in their care, listened to them more attentively and enjoyed them more; offered more support to children's conflict resolution skills and group-entry skills; were more patient and expressed less hostility during routine care; and offered greater support during children's emotional arousal. Caregivers of older toddlers in the control group were significantly more offensive and punitive towards the children, offered less frequent positive interactions and support during emotional arousal, and promoted less frequently children's social skills.

Children in daycare centres that received the LtLT training tended to show greater social competence, less frequent aggressive behaviour and less social withdrawal than children in the daycare centres that did not participate in the training. However, these differences are not statistically significant. We suggest that for the programme to show a statistically significant effect on children's behaviour, the assessment of children's behaviour should take place some while after a change has occurred in the caregivers' behaviour, rather than immediately after the change in caregivers' behaviour took place.

The overall quality of care declined during the year in all daycare centres. We assume that this reflects the effect of the poor standards of care and poor work conditions in these centres, and the resulting staff burn-out effects over the year. While the decline in quality of care in the 'control group' was associated with an increase in offensive and punitive behaviour towards children, this was not the case in the 'intervention group'. It seems that the LtLT training served as a protective measure against the 'burn-out' effect of year-long work in poor-quality centres.

Some concluding comments

The LtLT programme has evolved over the past 12 years, as changes were introduced following feedback from group facilitators and from participants. As the format and content of training have consolidated, the programme is currently being extended to meet new challenges. The first is adapting it to the Arab community in Israel. The second involves adapting the training (and its accompanying training materials) to professional teachers working with pre-school and kindergarten children.

Our informal interviews with participants in the programme, as well as the findings of the evaluation study, lead us to several conclusions, as follows.

Training early years practitioners to intervene in specific ways during social and emotional events at daycare can be effective in changing their interactions with children, and may thus have an effect on the evolving social and emotional competence of young children.

Social policy influences structural aspects of childcare quality. These in turn may either enhance, or limit, the effectiveness of the LtLT training. In poor-quality centres, as caregivers need to operate day after day in very stressful conditions leading to 'burn-out' effects, as well as difficulties in regulating their own emotions, the effectiveness of training may be rather limited.

To foster social and emotional competence – in high-quality childcare settings, as well as in poor-quality ones – caregivers' naturally occurring sensitive responsiveness and warmth need to be supplemented by other, more specific, interventions during the many daily social learning opportunities offered by the group-care context.

Culture-based beliefs and values concerning the meaning of social and emotional competence and the ways of achieving such competence are deeply ingrained. Training that aims to change the behaviour of caregivers must address these beliefs and values. Addressing culture-based beliefs and values is of special importance in multicultural childcare settings.

Point for reflection and discussion

Rosenthal and Gatt highlight the 'audience phenomenon' in peer groups, which gives extra responsibility to practitioners. Think of three different examples of powerful social-learning opportunities in daycare settings where children observe as an audience.

Note

1 The Learning to Live Together programme described in this chapter is one of initiatives of the Graduate programme of Early Childhood Studies at the Hebrew University in Jerusalem where Miriam Rosenthal and Lihi Gatt are based. This university department has been highly involved

for over 30 years in attempts to improve quality of care in Israeli daycare through: research that documents different aspects of children's and staff experience in daycare settings; the development of research-based training models and intervention programmes aiming at improving quality of care; and through attempts to change social policy related to childcare.

Bibliography

Arnett, J. (1989) 'Caregivers in day care centers: does training matter?' *Journal of Applied Developmental Psychology,* 10: 541–52.

Beer, T. (2007) 'Fostering social-emotional competence in young children in the educational setting: the caregiver's role'. Submitted thesis, The Hebrew University, Israel.

Davidov, M. and Grusec, J.E. (2006) 'Untangling the links of parental responsiveness to distress and warmth to child outcomes'. *Child Development,* 77: 44–58.

Denham, S.A. (1998) *Emotional Development in Young Children. The Guilford Series on Social and Emotional Development.* New York: Guilford Press.

Denham, S.A., Blair, K.A., DeMulder, E. *et al.* (2003) 'Preschool emotional competence: pathway to social competence?' *Child Development,* 74: 238–56.

Dunn, J. (2000) 'Mind-reading, emotion understanding, and relationships'. *International Journal of Behavioral Development,* 24: 142–4.

Furman, M. (1994) *The New Children: Violence and Obedience in Early Childhood.* Tel Aviv: Israel Hakibbutz Hameuchad Publishing House Ltd (Hebrew).

Gatt, L. (1999) *Toddlers learn empathy; Toddlers learn to play together; Toddlers learn conflict resolution: Three training films of the 'Learning to live Together' program.* Jerusalem: The Hebrew University Multimedia Center.

——(2004) *Learning to Live Together: Guidebook.* Jerusalem: Hebrew University.

——(2005) 'The effect of video-aided supervision on caregivers' interactions with infants and toddlers'. Poster presented at the Society for Research in Child Development Biennial Meeting. Atlanta, April 2005.

——(2008) 'Video-aided supervision in early childhood centers: a narrative analysis of the supervisee's perspective'. Submitted thesis. The Hebrew University, Israel.

Greenfield, P.M., Keller, H., Fuligni, A.J. and Maynard, A. (2003) 'Cultural pathways through universal development'. *Annual Review of Psychology,* 54: 461–90.

Grusec, J.E. and Redler, E. (1980) 'Attribution, reinforcement, and altruism: a developmental analysis'. *Developmental Psychology,* 16: 525–34.

Harkness, S. and Super, C.M. (1996) *Parents' cultural belief systems.* New York: The Guilford Press.

Harms, T., Cryer, D. and Clifford, R.M. (2003) *Infant/Toddler Environment Rating Scale: Revised Edition.* New York: Teachers College Press.

Hoffman, M.L. (1984) 'Interaction of affect and cognition in empathy'. In C.E. Izard, J. Kagan and R.B. Zajonc (eds), *Emotions, Cognition, and Behavior.* Cambridge: Cambridge University Press, pp. 103–31.

Howes, C. (1980) 'Peer play scale as an index of complexity of peer interaction'. *Developmental Psychology,* 16: 371–2.

Howes, C. (2000) 'Social-emotional classroom climate in child care, child–teacher relationships, and children's second grade peer relations'. *Social Development,* 9: 191–204.

Howes, C., Matheson, C.C. and Hamilton, C.E. (1994) 'Maternal, teacher, and child care history correlates of children's relationships with peers', *Child Development,* 65: 264–73.

Kemple, K.M., David, G.H. and Hysmith, C. (1997) 'Teachers' interventions in preschool and kindergarten children's peer interaction'. *Journal of Research in Childhood Education,* 12: 34–47.

Klein, H. (1991) 'Temperament and childhood group care adjustment: a cross-cultural comparison'. *Early Childhood Research Quarterly*, 6: 211–24.

Kontos, S., Burchinal, M., Howes, C., Wisseh, S. and Galinsky, E. (2002) 'An eco-behavioral approach to examining the contextual effects of early childhood classrooms'. *Early Childhood Research Quarterly,* 17: 239–58.

Koren-Karie, N., Egoz, N., Sagi, A. *et al.* (1998) 'The emotional climate of center care in Israel'. Paper presented at the International Society for the Study of Behavioural Development, Bern, July 1998.

LaFreniere, P.J. and Dumas, J.E. (1996) 'Social competence and behavior evaluation in children ages 3 to 6 years: the short form (SCBE-30)'. *Psychological Assessment,* 8: 369–77.

NICHD (2001) 'Child care and children's peer interaction at 24 and 36 months: the NICHD study of early child care'. *Child Development,* 72: 1478–500.

Rosenthal, M.K. (1991) 'Behaviors and beliefs of caregivers in family daycare: the effects of background and work environment'. *Early Childhood Research Quarterly,* 6: 263–83.

——(1994) *An Ecological Approach to the Study of Child Care Family Day Care in Israel.* Hillsdale, N.J.: Lawrence Erlbaum.

——(2003) 'Quality in early childhood education and care: a cultural context'. *European Early Childhood Education Research Journal*, 11: 101–16.

Rosenthal, M.K. and Gatt, L. (in press) 'Learning to Live Together: Training early childhood educators to promote socio-emotional competence of toddlers and pre-school children', *European Early Childhood Education Research Journal*, 18(4).

Rosenthal, M.K., Gatt, L. and Zur, H. (2008) *Children are not born violent: the social and emotional life of very young children.* Tel Aviv: Israel Hakibbutz Hameuchad Publishing House Ltd (Hebrew).

Rosenthal, M.K. and Roer-Strier, D. (2001) 'Cultural differences in mothers' developmental goals and ethnotheories'. *International Journal of Psychology,* 36: 20–31.

——(2006) 'What sort of an adult would you like your child to be? Mothers' developmental goals in different cultural communities in Israel'. *International Journal of Behavioral Development,* 30: 517–28.

Rosenthal, M.K. and Zur, H. (1993) 'The relationship between caregivers' interventions during peer interaction and toddlers' expression of concern for others'. Paper presented at the Society for Research in Child Development, New Orleans, 1993.

Sroufe, L.A., Schork, E., Motti, F., Lawrosky, N. and LaFreniere, P. (1984) 'The role of affect in social competence'. In C.E. Izard, J. Kagan and R.B. Zajonc (eds) *Emotions, Cognition, and Behavior.* Cambridge, England: Cambridge University Press.

Tobin, J., Wu, D. and Davidson, D. (1989) *Preschool in Three Cultures.* New Haven, C.T.: Yale University Press.

Zadok, I. (2005) 'Ethics, values and survival: a caregiver's role as seen by caregivers in Early childhood settings in Israel'. Submitted thesis. The Hebrew University, Israel.

Zur, H. (2002) 'The beliefs and knowledge of caregivers in family daycare regarding toddlers' social behavior'. Submitted thesis. The Hebrew University, Israel.

Chapter 11

Respect

Principles and practice in adult education in an early childhood setting in Mexico

Roxanna Pastor Fasquelle[1]

Introduction

In Mexico most families who send their children to daycare do so because they need to work and do not have extended family nearby who can take care of the children. The public institutions such as the Social Security Institute for State Workers (ISSSTE), the Mexican Social Security Institute (IMSS) and the Ministry of Public Education (SEP) offer this free service to a small percentage of the population as a benefit for women workers who otherwise could not come to work. This situation shapes the type and quality of care that is offered. The daycare centres tend to be big facilities that can give service to 100 to 200 children. Classrooms for children under the age of three will usually have between ten and twenty children, and classrooms for pre-schoolers between twenty and thirty with two childcare workers.

Both families and institutions are primarily concerned with the safety of the children during the day and a great deal of effort and resources are put into this. Children can attend group care from the moment they are three months old until they turn six years old when they can enter elementary (primary) school. The service is provided for nine to twelve hours per day in direct relationship to the mothers' work schedule. The children receive two complete meals and each daycare centre has a doctor, nurse, nutritionist, psychologist, social worker and pedagogue who supervise the well-being of the children. The direct care of the children is undertaken by childcare workers whose main reference is being mothers and who have many years of experience in the field. The majority of them have secondary level education and just a few have some vocational level training in childcare. Due to a recent change in the law, the pre-school level childcare workers must have a bachelors degree in education, but the number of workers who have this level of qualification is still small.

Most children who attend this type of care spend between seven and eight hours with their childcare providers and their peers. The majority of them will remain in the same daycare centre between four and six years. Although the entrance to group care can be difficult for some children, once they adapt most of them have a joyful experience. They tend to be very social children with close relationships with their providers and a great capacity to participate in group activities, play with others and be self-sufficient in their daily care. However, given the number of children in the group and the little understanding that the childcare workers have of child development and the role of play, children as young as six months are expected to adapt to group norms and learn through direct instruction. Play is something children do as a reward 'once the work (directed activities) is finished' and after lunch once the daily 'pedagogical activities' are done. As a consequence, although children do spend plenty of time playing, caregivers are not involved in their play nor do they see it as an opportunity for learning.

Given the social nature of the service, the training of the caregivers has not been a high priority. This chapter describes an on-site training programme for childcare providers who work in public institutions that offer daycare services to the children of government employees. For the past eight years the programme has been implemented in four different daycare sites in Mexico City and 34 providers have been trained.

The programme has been designed by the author and implemented by the same in collaboration with her masters degree students of the Mexican National Autonomous University (UNAM) Graduate School of Psychology. It was designed after many years of training students in these types of daycare centres and not seeing any long-term effects in the childcare workers' practices. The main challenges were how to provide basic knowledge on child development and assessment to women with very little formal education, how to teach them the value of observation and reflection of their daily practices, and how to attend to their needs as providers for large groups of children under the age of six.

The result is a 52-week programme that provides basic theoretical knowledge of child development through a weekly workshop, establishes an ongoing relationship between a child development specialist and each childcare worker who work side by side in the classroom, and provides ample opportunity to reflect on their practices, their knowledge and their attitudes. A self-evaluation instrument of developmentally appropriate practices was designed and serves as a guide for the childcare providers and the masters degree students.

The graduate placement: promoting child development in the first years of life

The graduate placement serves as the practicum for the masters level degree in educational psychology at UNAM. The graduate students are psychologists who wish to work as early childhood specialists. The practicum consists of a two-year placement in a daycare centre that serves children from birth to six years of age. Core elements of this internship are: (1) relationship-based learning (Casper and Theilheimer 2000); (2) emphasis on critical and reflective practice (Fenichel 1992); (3) supportive learning environments; (4) classes on child development, assessment and intervention with children under the age of six, their families and caregivers; (5) adult education and learning; and (6) a field placement that requires students to work inside the daycare classrooms, engage in a teaching and learning relationship with the caregivers as a mentor, and be involved in direct work with children and their families.

Copyright Jon Spaull/Bernard van Leer Foundation

The biggest challenge faced by the graduate students is learning how to relate, learn from and facilitate the learning of the childcare workers. Coming from an academic setting, where formal education is often seen as the most valuable and sometimes the only knowledge, they need to change their attitudes and acquire the knowledge and skills necessary to teach adults.

The on-site training programme for childcare providers

The on-site training programme is carried out during the second school year when the graduate students have acquired sufficient theoretical knowledge of both child development and adult learning theories, and have established relationships with the childcare providers and an understanding of their needs and resources as well as the particulars of the daycare centre. The programme's key perspectives are based on eight principles of adult learning (Vella 2002), as described below.

Intervention must be based on a needs assessment and participants must have an active participation in the process

In this programme the needs assessment is conducted in three different ways: the graduate students who will carry out the training spend time in the classrooms and observe the care and educational practices of the childcare workers; the childcare workers self-evaluate their practices at the beginning, the middle and the end of the training; the graduate student and the childcare worker have a dialogue about these results and choose those practices and areas that are a priority for the childcare worker.

Once all the participants have carried out the needs assessment, the trainers make sure that the needs and interests of the childcare workers are taken into account in the content and method of the programme.

In conjunction with the above, both graduate students and childcare workers identify on a weekly basis their abilities and needs. This information shapes the work of the following week. At the beginning, identifying one's own needs is not easy. Both the graduate students and the childcare workers come from traditional educational settings where the teachers decide what the students must learn. However, having a list of appropriate practices (see self-evaluation instrument p. 134) guides this initial stage and reflecting on one's own needs in a weekly basis becomes a habit.

Sound relationships must be established between trainers and participants

This is one of the founding principles of the programme. Vella (2002) mentions that a sound relationship for learning must include respect, listening and humility. This is applied in the following manner.

Respect Establishing relationships between the university team and the childcare providers who come from different realities and educational backgrounds, involves learning to value and respect differences. This can be very challenging for both sides. At the beginning the childcare workers feel threatened by the presence of the graduate students in their classrooms given that previous experience with 'professionals' is one of disrespect for their work. On the other hand, the graduate students feel insecure in this new role and often deal with this feeling by having to know all the answers. Here the role of the university supervisor as someone who feels at ease in the childcare settings and who respects and values the knowledge of the childcare workers is fundamental. Most of the supervisor's time during the first semester is spent establishing relationships with the graduate students, with the childcare providers and helping build bridges between the two.

Listening 'But what was she or he saying?' This is one of the key questions posed to the students and myself. Listening implies reflecting about what one hears and observes. Too often we tend to judge the words and actions of others instead of listening. All of the graduate students identify 'active listening' as a key skill and attitude they acquire in this programme.

Humility In this programme humility primarily means saying, 'I don't know but we can try to find an answer together'. This is difficult because both the childcare worker and the graduate student strongly believe that a good professional must have all the answers. This erroneous idea is what shapes their relationship at the beginning. The childcare worker expects answers to all his/her problems and the graduate student feels she or he should have them. Once the graduate student can say for the first time, 'I don't know but we can try to find an answer together' the spell is broken and they begin to see each other as human beings who can construct knowledge together.

A safe learning environment built on trust and a non-judgemental approach

Trust in the competence of the design and the teachers By the time this training programme starts the graduate students who will conduct the training have spent a good deal of time in the childcare classrooms working side by side with the caregivers, learning from them and sharing their knowledge. More importantly, the childcare workers know that the graduate students have an understanding of the childcare settings and their needs.

Trust in the feasibility and relevance of the objectives Since the childcare workers participate in the needs assessment they trust that their needs are taken into consideration. The fact that the training is carried out on site with the support of the daycare centre's programme director and the supervisors, assures the participants that the training is directly linked with what their workplace demands from them.

A non-judgemental environment This implies making sure that the way the training is carried out recognizes the childcaregivers' knowledge, perspectives and needs. Learning to listen and to understand where a particular response might be coming from is one of the key challenges faced by the university team.

Praxis: ample opportunity to reflect on their practice

This is taught in a variety of ways. The first is through an ongoing dialogue between the childcare provider and the graduate student assigned to her classroom. The two have an ongoing conversation about the day's events. Speaking through the child and the childcare provider's behaviour is a useful technique for inviting the provider to reflect on her actions.

The weekly workshop begins by asking the participants to reflect on their week: 'what did you do, how did it go, what did you learn and how did you feel?' are guiding questions. During the session participants are often eager to share their thoughts, their experiences, their opinions and their questions. A recurring comment from the university team is 'but why do you think or feel that way? Or why do you think that happened?' Participants often laugh and say, 'I know, I know you want to know why'.

A useful strategy to help both graduate students and childcare providers is a diary in which they can reflect on that week's work. As a product of this reflection they identify the knowledge, skills and attitudes they are acquiring and what they need for their learning. The childcare workers share their reflections with their mentor.

Sequence and reinforcement

These two elements shape the content and method of the programme. Introducing concepts and skills from the simple to the complex and giving ample opportunity for practice and integration implies an initial design and an ongoing modification of the training workshops and classroom work. At the end of each workshop the team meets to discuss whether the objectives were accomplished and if the participants could understand and apply the concepts, and decisions are made to guide the follow-up work in the classrooms and modify if necessary the following workshop. At the end of each week the team meets again to comment on the classroom work. What worked, what didn't and what needs to be addressed again.

Respect for learners as decision makers

Vella (2002: 16) sums up this principle by saying 'Don't ever do what the learner can do; don't ever decide what the learner can decide'. For people coming from traditional educational backgrounds where the teacher 'knows best' this is a difficult practice. It requires ongoing observation, dialogue and trust. One must remain alert and install practices that help both the trainers and the caregivers to have clear roles and not overstep their boundaries. One of them is asking participants to identify their strengths and needs on a regular basis, and making sure the contents of the programme respond to what the childcare providers are saying they want and need to learn.

At times the graduate student thinks and feels the priorities established by the childcare provider are not adequate for what he or she is observing in the classroom. Learning to listen and understand the provider's point of view is an ongoing challenge as well as learning to share his or her thoughts and observations with the provider so he/she can consider his or her point of view. This is especially difficult at the beginning when it is common for childcare providers to ask their mentor to make decisions for them. This requires the graduate student to step back and create the necessary conditions to help the learners make the decision or to make a joint decision. For example, when the graduate student does not agree with the way a childcare worker responds to a child who 'misbehaves' and the response of the childcare provider is 'tell me what to do with her', the graduate student must invite the childcare provider to observe and reflect and not tell her what she should do, even when that is what the childcare worker expects and it may be an easier immediate solution.

Learning must include ideas, feelings and actions

Research findings show that acquiring information is not enough to produce a change of action or attitude. We need to teach in ways that help people to think and to feel whatever emotion it involves and to do something with it. Coming from an academic world it is easier to share knowledge than to understand people's feelings and attitudes. It is even more difficult to realize that it is our responsibility to create the necessary conditions for that new knowledge to generate changes in educational practices.

This programme's impact is measured by observing the childcare workers' daily practices with their children, reading their reflections and carrying out a dialogue with them. All of this helps understand what promotes or limits a participant's learning.

The first time the module of working with families was implemented, feelings were not taken into account. Since the providers often said they did not work with the families because they did not know how and did not have enough time, diverse strategies were discussed and help was offered to plan and carry out the activities. It didn't take more than a few minutes of listening to realize that what really prevented the childcare providers from seeing the families as their allies were the attitudes they had towards the families. In order to explore their concept of 'families' and how it might influence their perception of working parents, they were asked to share pictures and feelings of their families of origin. Understanding how their own experience influenced the way they related to the parents of the children they took care of was the first step. Now the module includes three sessions in which they work with the feelings, ideas and attitudes before learning strategies for working with families.

Immediacy: adult learners need to find an answer to the challenges they face on a daily basis

The childcare workers want to know how to deal with a child who won't listen like the others, how to help a child who should be talking and doesn't use words, or how to discipline a group of pre-schoolers who love to challenge authority. For many years I thought, 'If they knew child development they would understand the child's behaviour and would know what to do'. I now know that child development knowledge is just part of the story. I also know that they don't want to know as much about child development as I do. They want to solve their problems!

This programme attends to that need by working with childcare workers in their classrooms, talking about the challenges they face and incorporating those needs into the programme's contents. Most of the 'daily problems' can indeed be understood from a developmental perspective. However, the 'problem' can only be addressed if once it is understood they can make a plan to intervene and evaluate the results. This creates a new challenge. How to carry out a programme that responds to the individual needs of the participants?

The content must address what a childcare worker needs to know, understand and do to provide quality care and promote child development. But the programme also needs to ensure that each childcare provider has the time, space and support to address her particular needs and challenges. We do this through the weekly presence in the classrooms and the weekly meetings between the mentor and the provider. Attending to these immediate needs makes all the difference. It does not necessarily mean that the problems will be solved; it just means that they are being taken care of. The objective is to establish a link between the problems faced in the classrooms and the theory and exercises being addressed in the workshops and reading materials.

Copyright Jon Spaull/Bernard van Leer Foundation

Programme components

The programme has five major components, as described below.

An evaluation of the educational practices at the beginning, the middle and the end of the programme

The evaluation of the childcare worker's practices is done with 'Prácticas Apropiadas al Desarrollo. Un Instrumento de Auto-Evaluación' ('Developmentally Appropriate Practices. A Self-Evaluation Instrument') (Pastor 2001) – a Likert-type scale that includes the basic educational practices that must take place in a developmentally appropriate programme. The instrument is divided in five sections: (a) daily routines, (b) programme planning, (c) nurturing relationships, (d) physical environment, (e) materials. It has three different versions: (I) birth to 18 months, (II) 18 to 36 months, and (III) three to six years of age. The evaluation is carried out both by the provider and the graduate student who accompanies her in this process.

An 'acompañamiento' during the whole programme

A graduate student accompanies each childcare provider during the whole programme. The mentor gives individualized attention by working side by side with the childcare provider both in her classroom and in the weekly workshop. This includes sharing information and educational strategies according to her level of development, her immediate needs and whatever challenges she is facing in her classroom. The childcare workers, who are most often women, who care for [too] many people in their everyday lives and who are seldom cared for by others, consider this element the most important component for their learning.

A three-hour workshop that takes place once a week over a 52-week period

The theoretical component of the programme is addressed in a three-hour workshop that takes place every week. In these workshops themes are explored such as: child development, observation and documentation; differences between the role of a mother and the childcare provider; the basic principles and characteristics of an emotionally safe learning environment; assessment of children's learning and development and planning of the programme; and families as partners.

The weekly follow up

In order to put into practice the contents of the workshop and create a link between each childcare provider's needs and the theory, the graduate student works with the childcare provider inside her classroom. Each mentor spends at least one day per week in his or her partner's classroom. This allows the graduate student to know the children, the childcare workers and the challenges they face. In this time the mentor models some of the skills and attitudes the programme is trying to teach, for example: turning daily routines into learning opportunities.

A weekly diary in which every childcare provider reflects on her actions and learning

One of the two main learning strategies in this programme is to reflect on one's actions. Childcare workers work long hours and seldom stop to reflect on their actions. Making a habit of reflection is one of the outcomes of this programme. Childcare workers learn to reflect on their actions, identify their knowledge, their skills and their attitudes. Understanding this allows them to change what needs to be changed and to systematize what works.

Results and limitations

The programme has been implemented in three daycare centres with three groups of childcare providers and university students. Educational practices at the beginning, the middle and the end of the programme in all three centres have been evaluated using a variety of approaches. The results show that: (1) all childcare providers acquire most of the developmentally appropriate practices included in the self-evaluation instrument, and by the end of the programme most of them carry out these practices in a systematic way; (2) the practices that are not acquired are those that the daycare centres' policies do not support, for example the adult:child ratios are impossible due to the size of the groups; (3) all care providers understand that observation of the children and reflection on their practice are key qualities of a good childcare provider; (4) all providers assume the importance of their role in the well-being and development of the children and relate to them in a more healthy and respectful manner; (5) due to their educational backgrounds most childcare providers acquire limited knowledge of child development, but they do apply that knowledge in the work with the children and the set up of their classrooms; (6) most childcare providers understand the importance of working with the families for the well-being of the children, but how much they change their practices is influenced by the daycare policies of the institution; (7) the importance of the assessment and evaluation continuum is understood and carried out as long as the daycare centre does not demand from them a different type of planning or assessment procedure.

In Mexico most of the childcare workers have ample experience but little formal schooling. Rather than demanding a university level education, Mexico needs to put into place an accreditation system that, along with the right kind of training approach, can elevate the quality of care. The results of the programme described in this chapter show that an on-site training programme from a developmental perspective that attends to individual and group needs is the right approach.

Point for reflection and discussion

Pastor Fasquelle emphasizes the importance of mentoring and support of childcare workers. This involves having empathy with the childcare worker and understanding adult learning processes. Try to translate these insights into your own cultural context. Interview a childcare worker about her/his professional needs and expectations and how they can be best supported.

Note

1 Roxanna Pastor Fasquelle is professor at the Mexican National Autonomous University (UNAM) Graduate School of Psychology, Mexico City, where she has been working with trainee psychologists who want to be early childhood specialists. Her work and those of her colleagues includes assessment, evaluation and intervention from a developmental perspective with children, families, teachers and daycare settings. Attention is paid to working directly with children, teachers, families and communities.

Bibliography

Casper, V. and Theilheimer, R. (2000) 'Learning to teach others about working with infants, toddlers and families'. *Zero to Three*, 20: 6.

Day, C.B. (2004) *Essentials for Child Development Associates Working with Young Children.* Washington D.C.: Council for Professional Recognition.

Fenichel, E. (1992) *Learning through Supervision and Mentorship to Support the Development of Infants, Toddlers and their Families: A Source Book.* Washington, D.C.: Zero to Three.

NAEYC (1996) 'Developmentally appropriate practice in early childhood programs serving children from birth through age 8. A position statement of the National Association for the Education of Young Children'. In S. Bredekamp and C. Copple (eds) *Developmentally Appropriate Practice in Early Childhood Programs.* Washington, D.C.: NAEYC.

Pastor, R. (2001) *Prácticas Apropiadas al Desarrollo. Un Instrumento de Auto-Evaluación* [*Developmentally Appropriate Practices. A Self Evaluation Instrument*] Mexico: UNAM.

Vella, J. (2002) *Learning to Listen, Learning to Teach: The Power of Dialogue in Educating Adults.* San Francisco, C.A.: Jossey-Bass.

Index